SIGHT WORDS & SENTENCES

LEVEL 1:
EASY READING & WRITING PRACTICE FOR EARLY ELEMENTARY STUDENTS

LATE NOVEMBER LEARNING TREE

SIGHT WORDS & SENTENCES
Level 1: Easy Reading & Writing Practice for Early Elementary Students
BY LATE NOVEMBER LEARNING TREE

Published by Late November Literary
Winston Salem, NC 27107

ISBN: 979-8-9892723-4-1

Library of Congress Cataloging-in-Publication Data:
Late November Learning Tree.
Sight Words & Sentences / Late November Learning Tree 1st ed.

Printed in the United States of America

High Quality Educational Workbooks From Late November Learning Tree:

- ✓ Paragraph Practice
- ✓ Writing Essays
- ✓ Journaling Is Writing Too
- ✓ Journaling Through Scripture
- ✓ Journaling For Kids
- ✓ Sight Words & Sentences Level 1
- ✓ Sight Words & Sentences Level 2
- ✓ Poetry Practice

Learn more at www.latenovemberliterary.com!

How to Use This Book:

This workbook is a great tool for practicing sight word recognition, reading fluency, and strengthening writing skills. The sight words on these pages are a compilation of Dolch sight words based on the most commonly used words in the English language. They are called sight words because many of them do not necessarily follow the rules of the English language, so they need to be learned on sight (or recall).

- ✓ Each section includes 10 sight words to practice.
- ✓ Within the section, the students will be able to practice a sight word on each page by reading a sample sentence and then writing their own.
    - o Sample sentences include sight words as well as simple sounding words.
    - o The sentences are repetitive with sight words being repeated often.
    - o Most sentences also contain a higher-level word for students to practice with their teacher.
    - o The teacher should model the sentence by reading it out loud, and then have the child read the words out loud using their finger to read each word.
- ✓ Use this workbook on its own or in connection with other ELA activities.
- ✓ Each sight word practice also includes flashcards and a *Draw It!* portion which allows the student to read a sentence with the sight word and draw what the sentence describes.
    - o This is a great extension activity that taps into the child's creativity and puts word meanings into visual expressions.

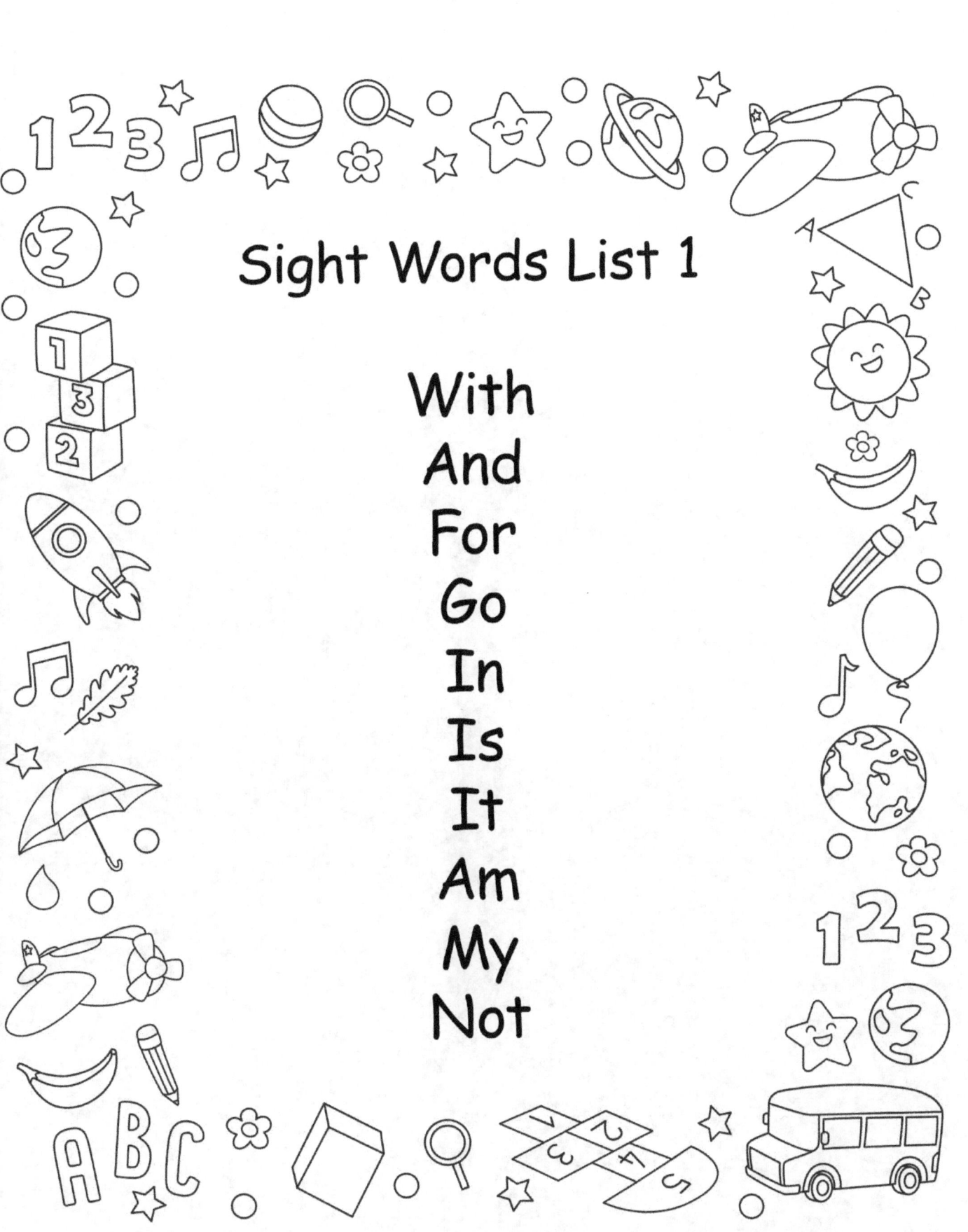

Sight Words List 1

With
And
For
Go
In
Is
It
Am
My
Not

Flashcard Practice:

with	and
for	go
in	is

it	am
my	not

Sight Word:

Practice Writing:

Can you write the word **with** in the box?

Sentence:

I go *with* you.

Your turn: Can you write your own sentence using **with**?

Draw It! Read the sentence and draw a picture of it.

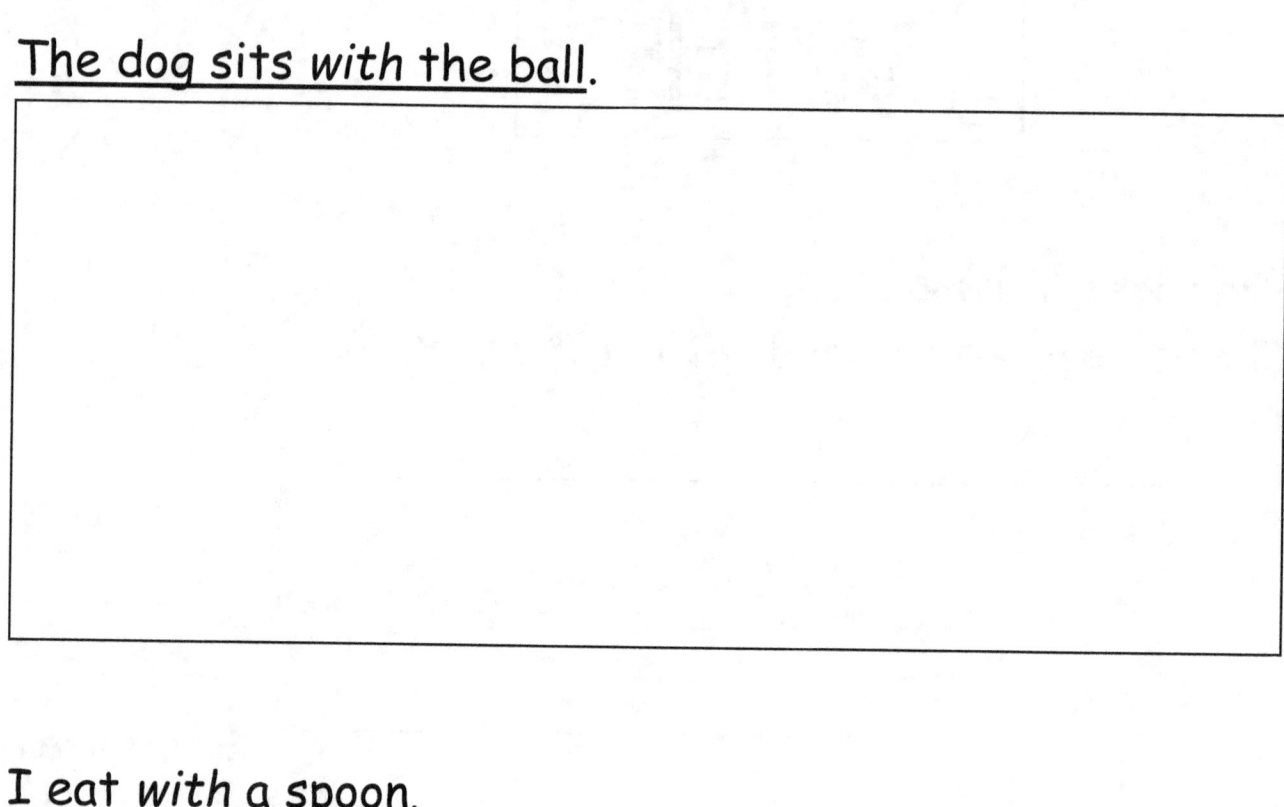

The dog sits _with_ the ball.

I eat _with_ a spoon.

Sight Word:

And

Practice Writing:

Can you write the word **and** in the box?

Sentence:

I like dogs *and* cats.

Your turn: Can you write your own sentence using **and**?

Draw It! Read the sentence and draw a picture of it.

The net has fish _and shells_.

The flower is red _and blue_.

Sight Word:

For

Practice Writing:

Can you write the word *for* in the box?

Sentence:

I can draw *for* you.

Your turn: Can you write your own sentence using *for*?

Draw It! Read the sentence and draw a picture of it.

<u>Here is a gift *for* you</u>.

<u>It is time *for* bed</u>.

Sight Word:

Go

Practice Writing:

Can you write the word *go* in the box?

Sentence:

I *go* to the store.

Your turn: Can you write your own sentence using *go*?

Draw It! Read the sentence and draw a picture of it.

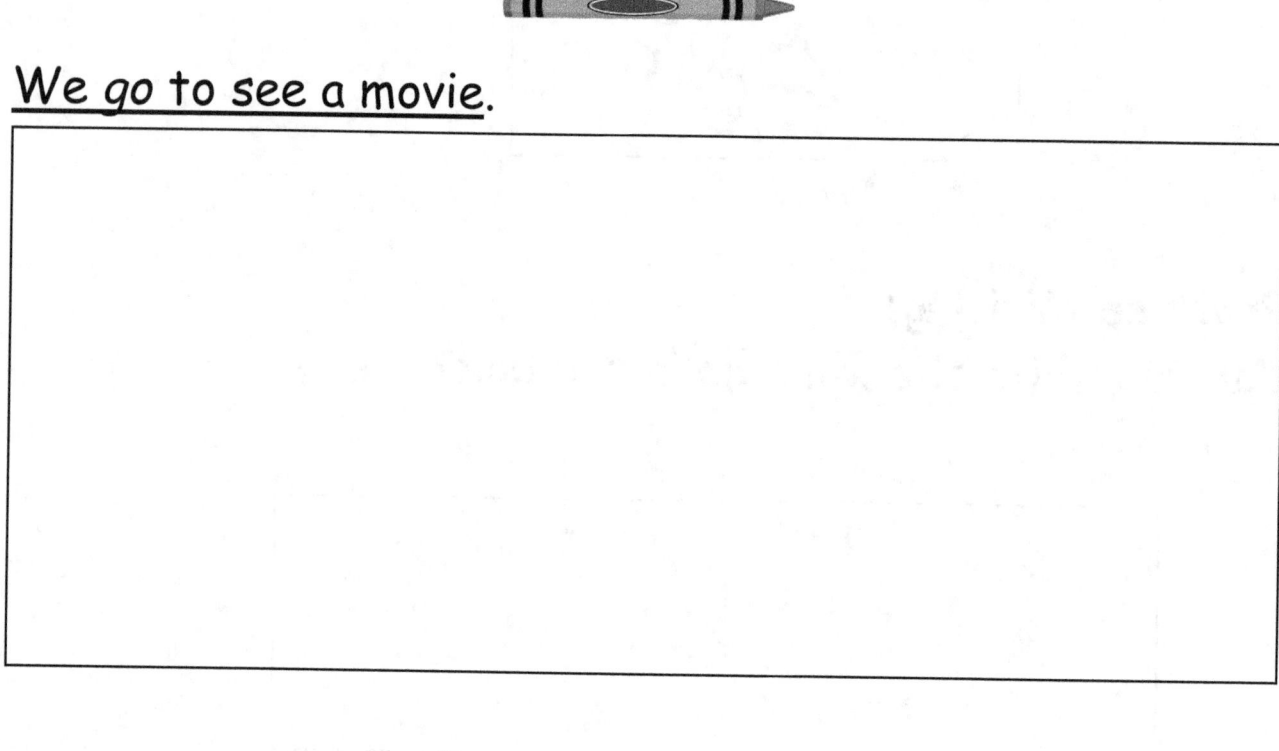

<u>We *go* to see a movie</u>.

<u>The car will *go* fast</u>.

Sight Word:

In

Practice Writing:

Can you write the word *in* in the box?

Sentence:

We go *in* the house.

Your turn: Can you write your own sentence using *in*?

Draw It! Read the sentence and draw a picture of it.

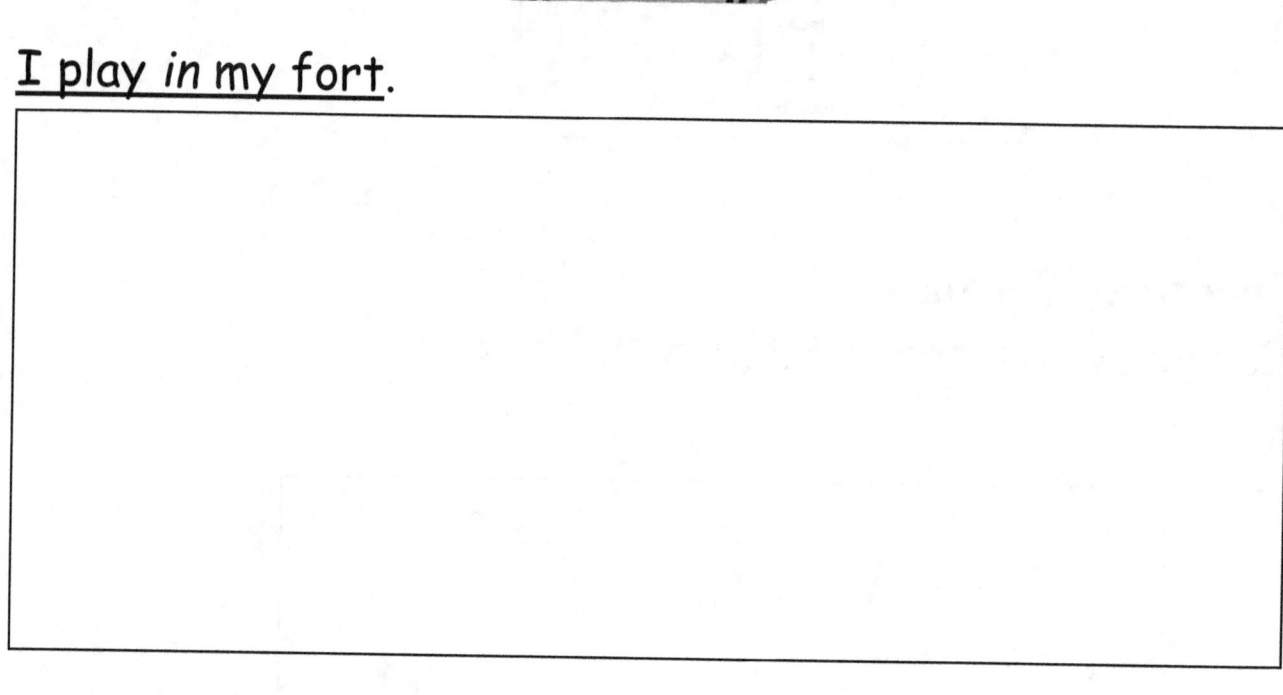

<u>I play *in* my fort</u>.

<u>I sing *in* my room</u>.

Sight Word:

Is

Practice Writing:

Can you write the word *is* in the box?

Sentence:

My dad *is* a builder.

Your turn: Can you write your own sentence using *is*?

Draw It! Read the sentence and draw a picture of it.

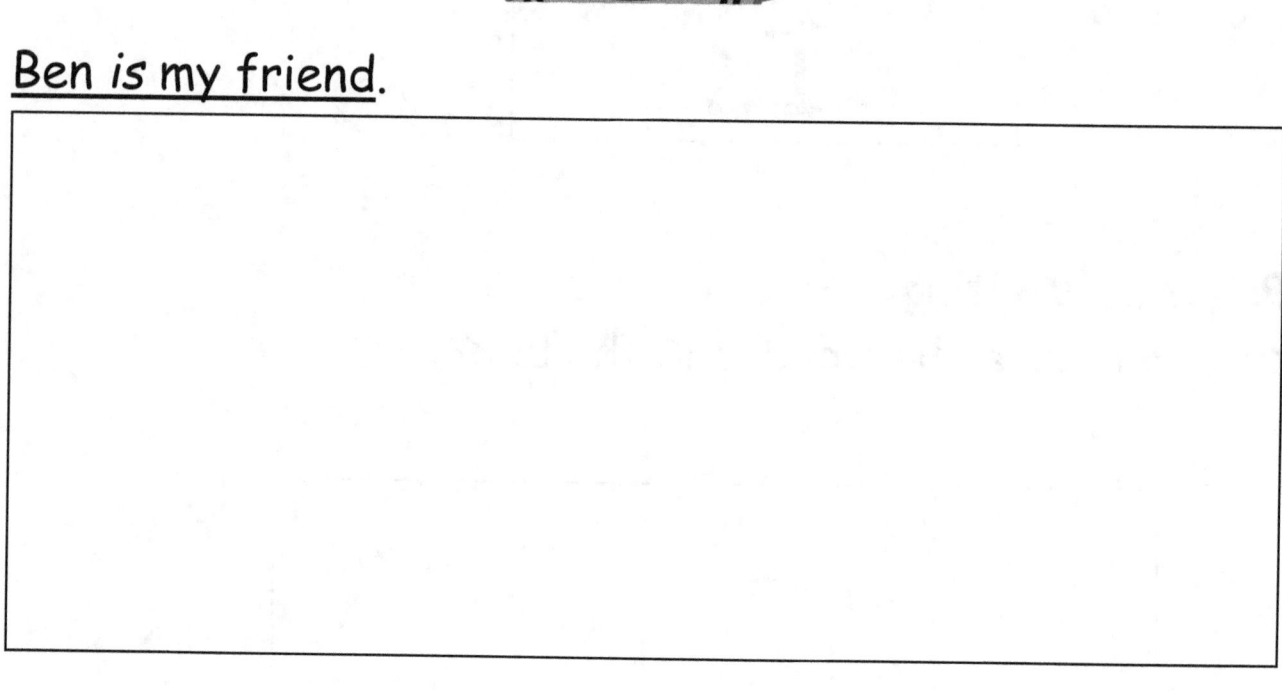

<u>Ben</u> *is* <u>my friend</u>.

<u>This</u> *is* <u>my mom</u>.

Sight Word:

It

Practice Writing:

Can you write the word *it* in the box?

Sentence:

It is warm outside.

Your turn: Can you write your own sentence using *it*?

Draw It! Read the sentence and draw a picture of it.

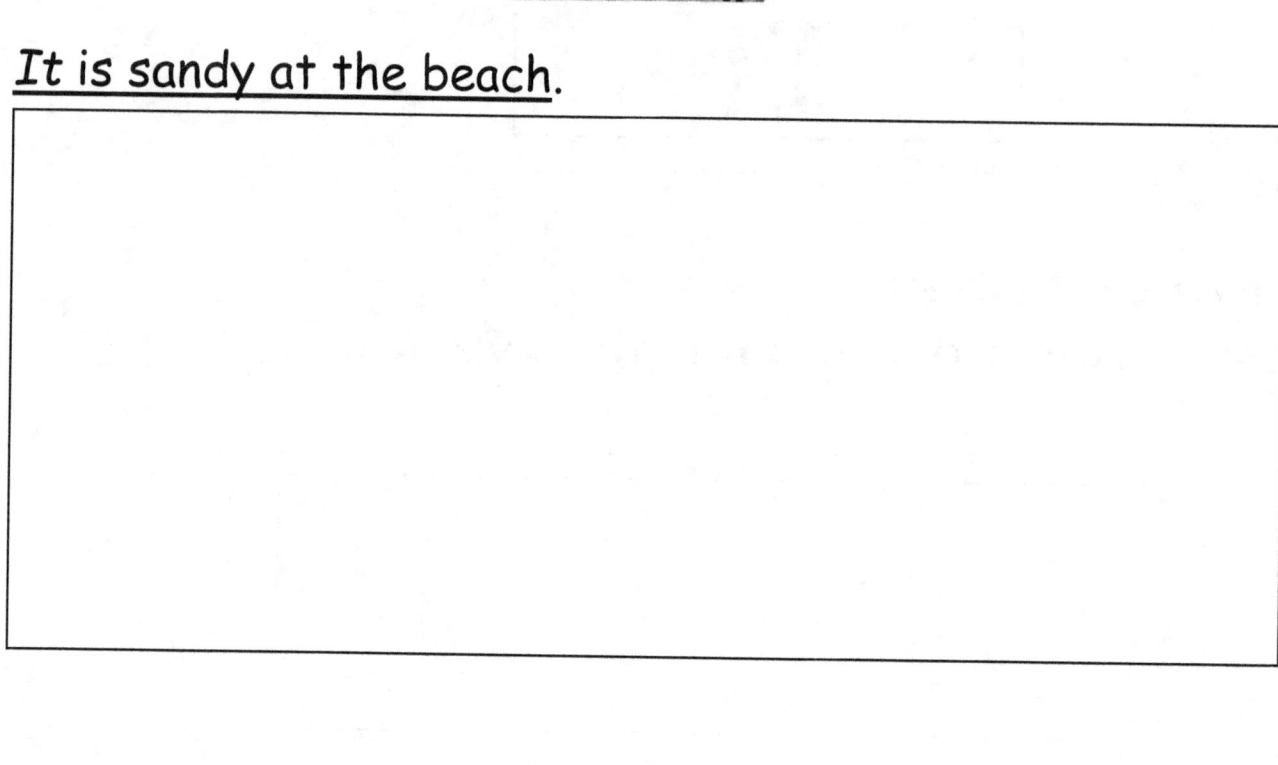

<u>It is sandy at the beach</u>.

<u>It is a funny face</u>.

Sight Word:

Am

Practice Writing:

Can you write the word **am** in the box?

Sentence:

I *am* at the car.

Your turn: Can you write your own sentence using **am**?

Draw It! Read the sentence and draw a picture of it.

<u>I am a fireman</u>.

<u>I am a doctor</u>.

Sight Word:

My

Practice Writing:

Can you write the word **my** in the box?

Sentence:

I love *my* pet turtle.

Your turn: Can you write your own sentence using **my**?

Draw It! Read the sentence and draw a picture of it.

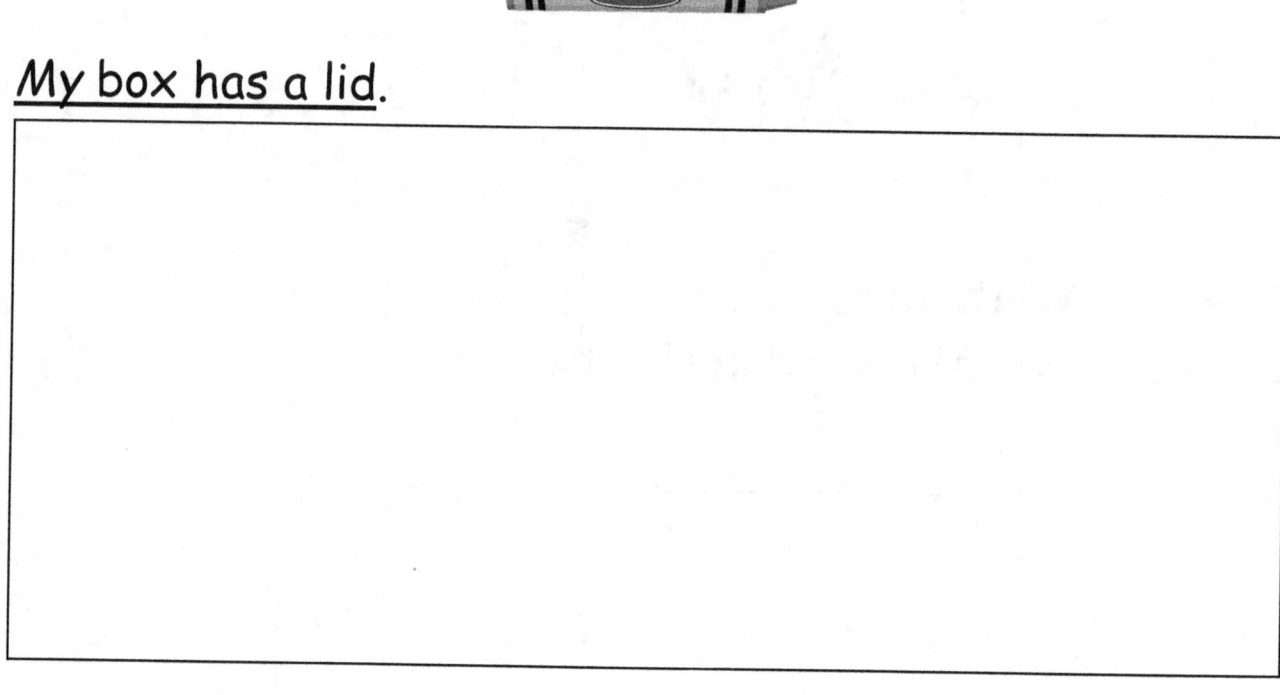

<u>My box has a lid</u>.

<u>This is my doll</u>.

Sight Word:

Not

Practice Writing:

Can you write the word **not** in the box?

Sentence:

We will *not* go to the park.

Your turn: Can you write your own sentence using **not**?

Draw It! Read the sentence and draw a picture of it.

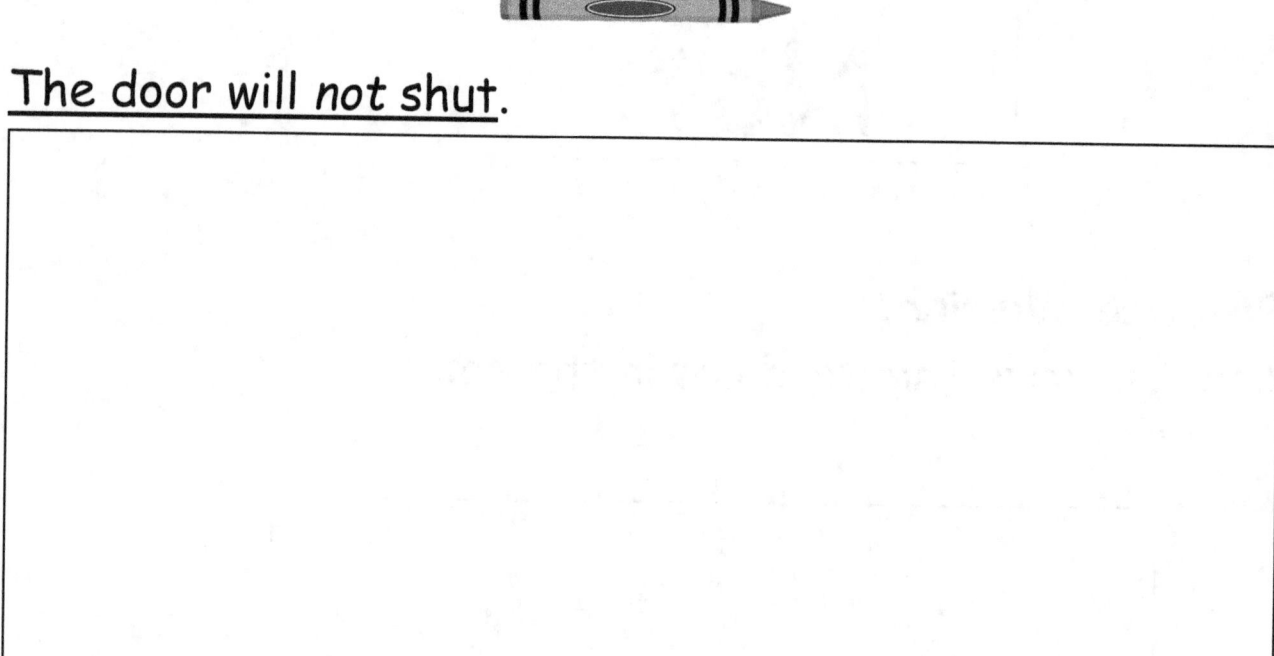

The door will *not* shut.

The water in my cup is *not* cold.

Sight Words List 2

Run
See
The
Up
Come
Went
Down
Big
Help
Can

Flashcard Practice:

run	see
the	up
come	went

down	big
help	can

Sight Word:

Run

Practice Writing:

Can you write the word **run** in the box?

Sentence:

I can *run* far.

Your turn: Can you write your own sentence using *run*?

Draw It! Read the sentence and draw a picture of it.

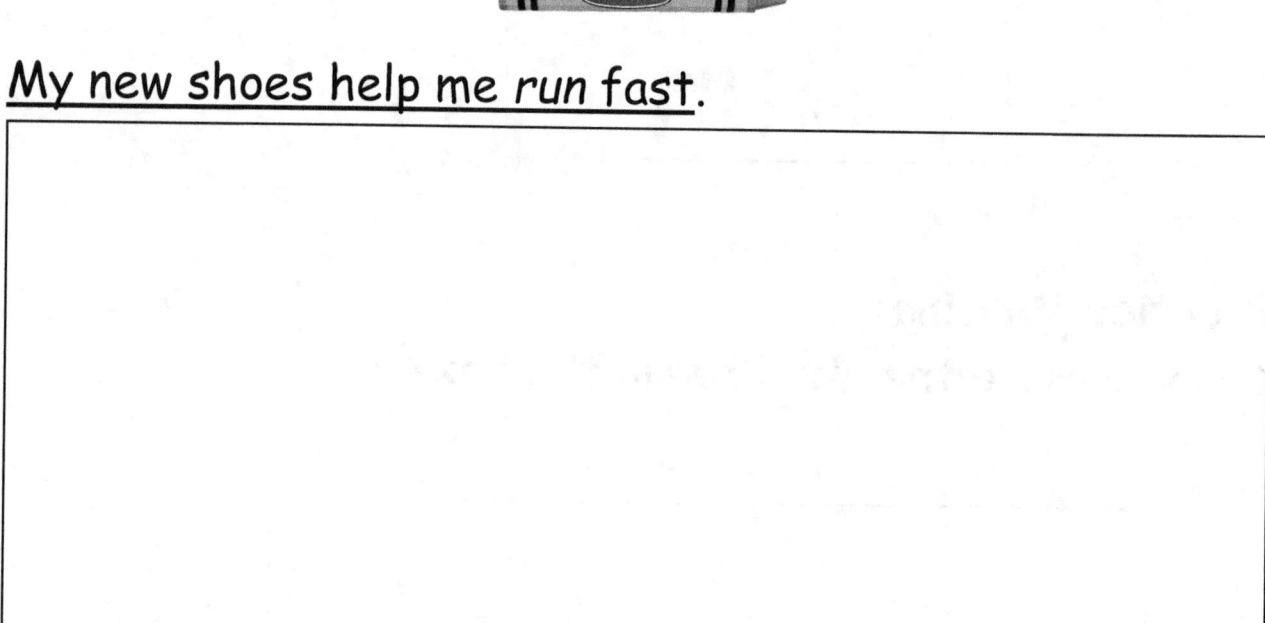

<u>My new shoes help me *run* fast</u>.

I want to *run* a race and win a prize.

Sight Word:

See

Practice Writing:

Can you write the word **see** in the box?

Sentence:

Do you *see* the blue bird in the tree?

Your turn: Can you write your own sentence using **see**?

Draw It! Read the sentence and draw a picture of it.

I see the mailman at the door.

I see a green balloon in the sky.

Sight Word:

The

Practice Writing:

Can you write the word *the* in the box?

Sentence:

The book is good.

Your turn: Can you write your own sentence using *the*?

Draw It! Read the sentence and draw a picture of it.

<u>*The* little girl picks flowers in the park</u>.

<u>I can see *the* moon at night</u>.

Sight Word:

Up

Practice Writing:

Can you write the word *up* in the box?

Sentence:

We go *up* the stairs.

Your turn: Can you write your own sentence using *up*?

Draw It! Read the sentence and draw a picture of it.

I like to look _up_ and see the stars.

The bird is _up_ in the tree.

Sight Word:

Come

Practice Writing:

Can you write the word **come** in the box?

Sentence:

We will *come* to the parade.

Your turn: Can you write your own sentence using **come**?

Draw It! Read the sentence and draw a picture of it.

The boy and girl come outside to play.

[box]

I will come inside the bakery for a sweet treat.

[box]

Sight Word:

Went

Practice Writing:

Can you write the word **went** in the box?

Sentence:

My family *went* to the farm.

Your turn: Can you write your own sentence using **went**?

Draw It! Read the sentence and draw a picture of it.

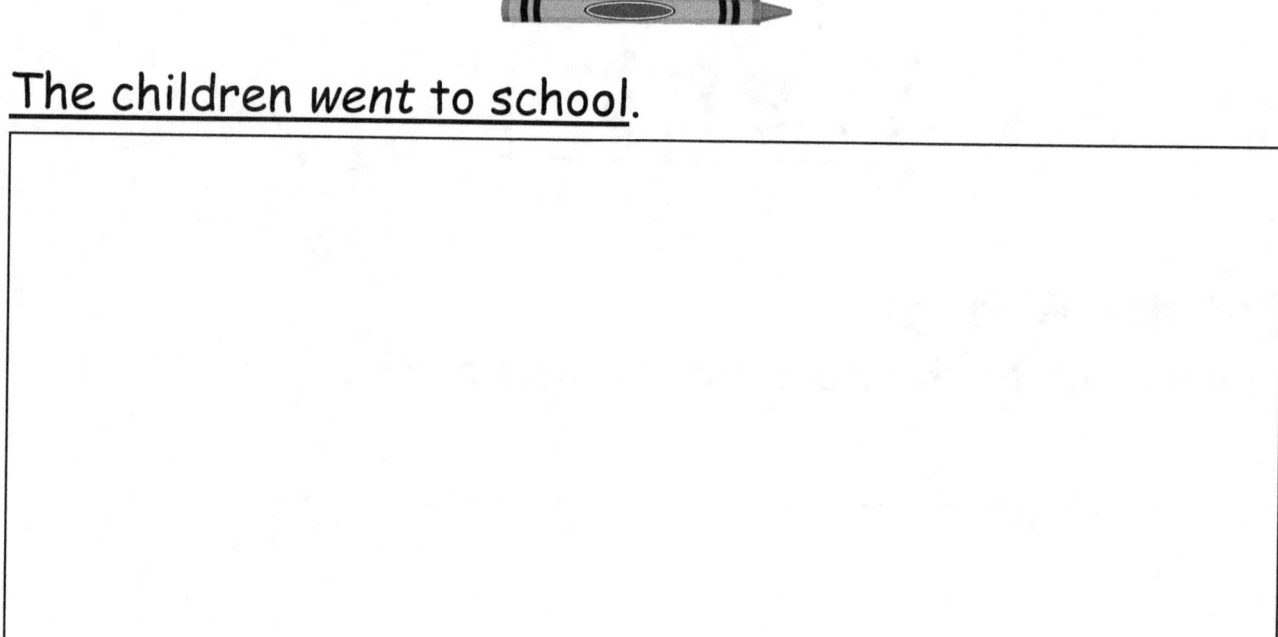

The children _went_ to school.

The rain _went_ away, and the sun came out.

Sight Word:

Down

Practice Writing:

Can you write the word *down* in the box?

Sentence:

We went *down* the stairs.

Your turn: Can you write your own sentence using *down*?

Draw It! Read the sentence and draw a picture of it.

The boy fell _down_ and hurt his leg.

Mom bent _down_ and gave me a hug.

Sight Word:

Big

Practice Writing:

Can you write the word *big* in the box?

Sentence:

The *big* truck is loud.

Your turn: Can you write your own sentence using *big*?

Draw It! Read the sentence and draw a picture of it.

We went to the *big* city to see the *big* buildings.

Our *big* dog likes to lick my face.

Sight Word:

Help

Practice Writing:

Can you write the word *help* in the box?

Sentence:

Can you *help* me with this?

Your turn: Can you write your own sentence using *help*?

Draw It! Read the sentence and draw a picture of it.

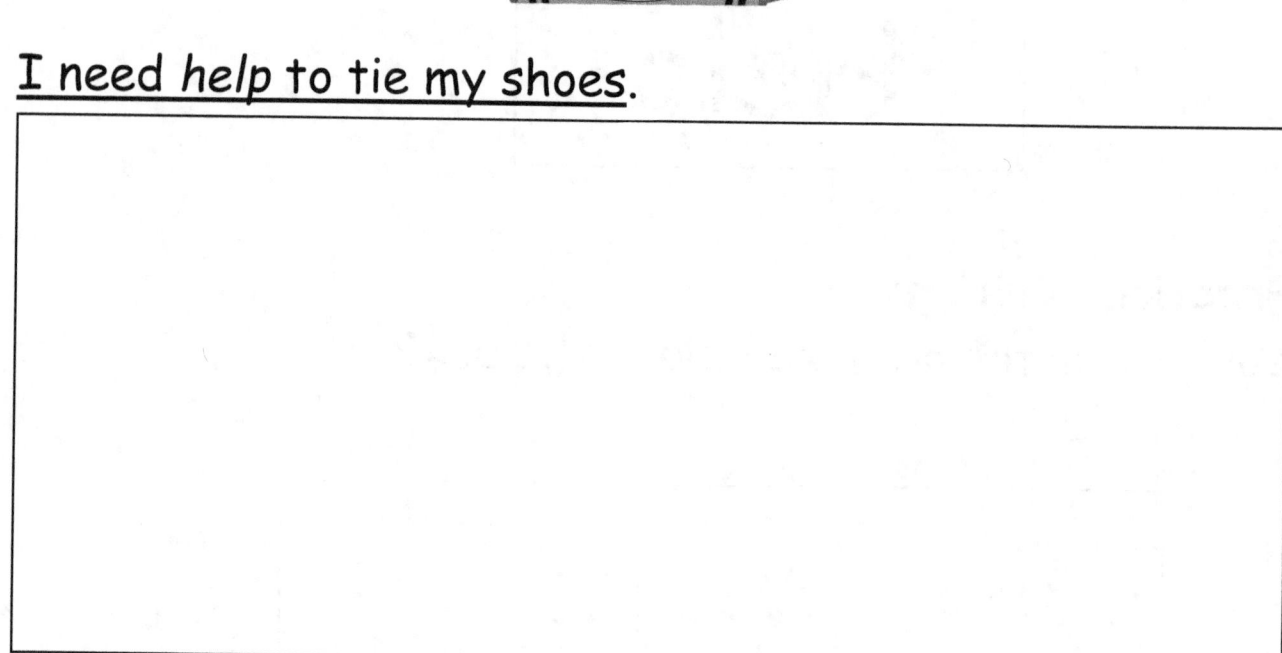

I need *help* to tie my shoes.

The fireman can *help* get my cat from the tree.

Sight Word:

Can

Practice Writing:

Can you write the word *can* in the box?

Sentence:

You *can* play with me.

Your turn: Can you write your own sentence using *can*?

Draw It! Read the sentence and draw a picture of it.

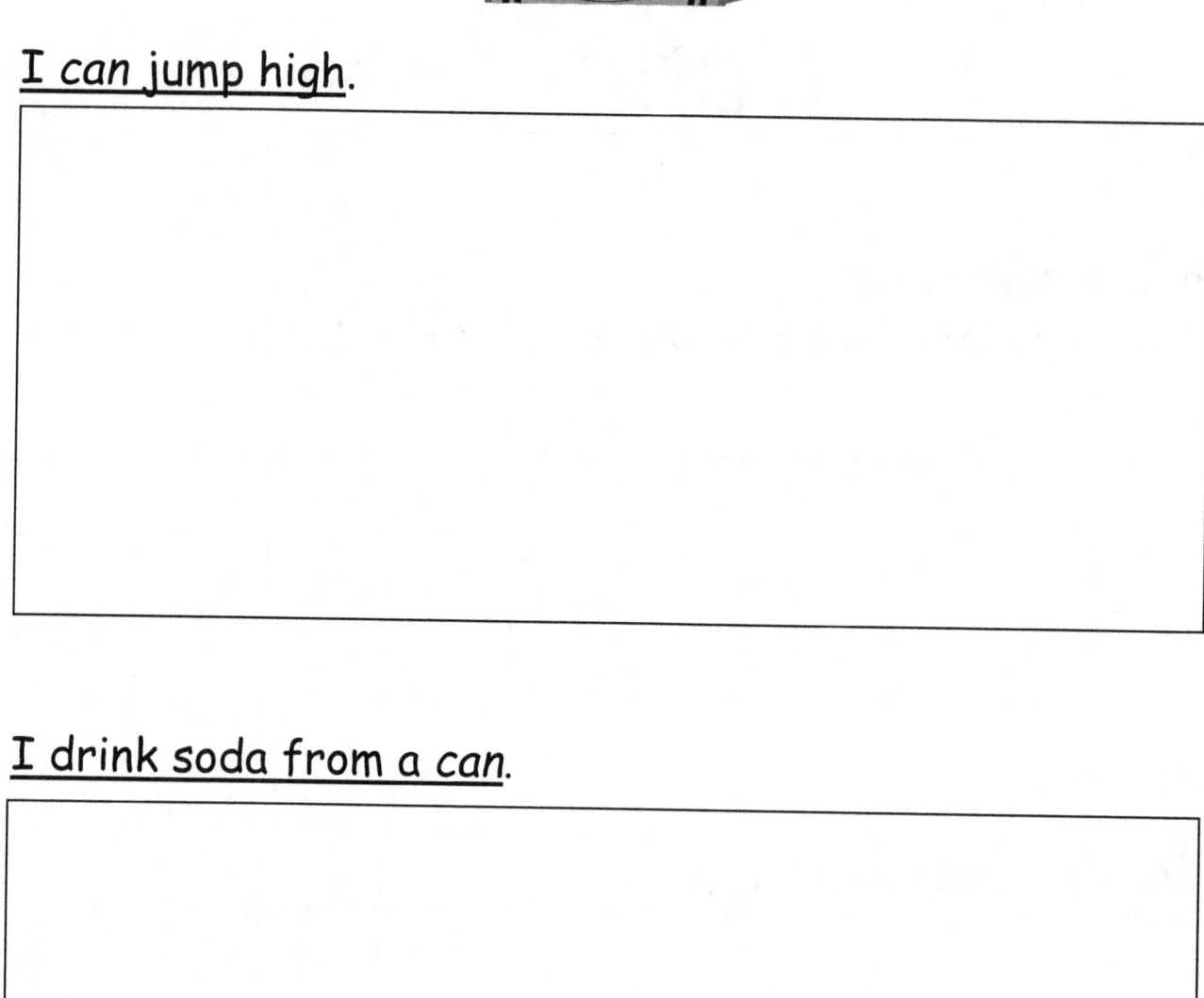

I <u>can</u> jump high.

I drink soda from a <u>can</u>.

Sight Words List 3

Said
Here
He
She
Our
We
They
Me
You
This

Flashcard Practice:

said	here
he	she
our	we

they	me
you	this

Sight Word:

Said

Practice Writing:

Can you write the word *said* in the box?

Sentence:

My mom *said* to pick up the toys.

Your turn: Can you write your own sentence using *said*?

Draw It! Read the sentence and draw a picture of it.

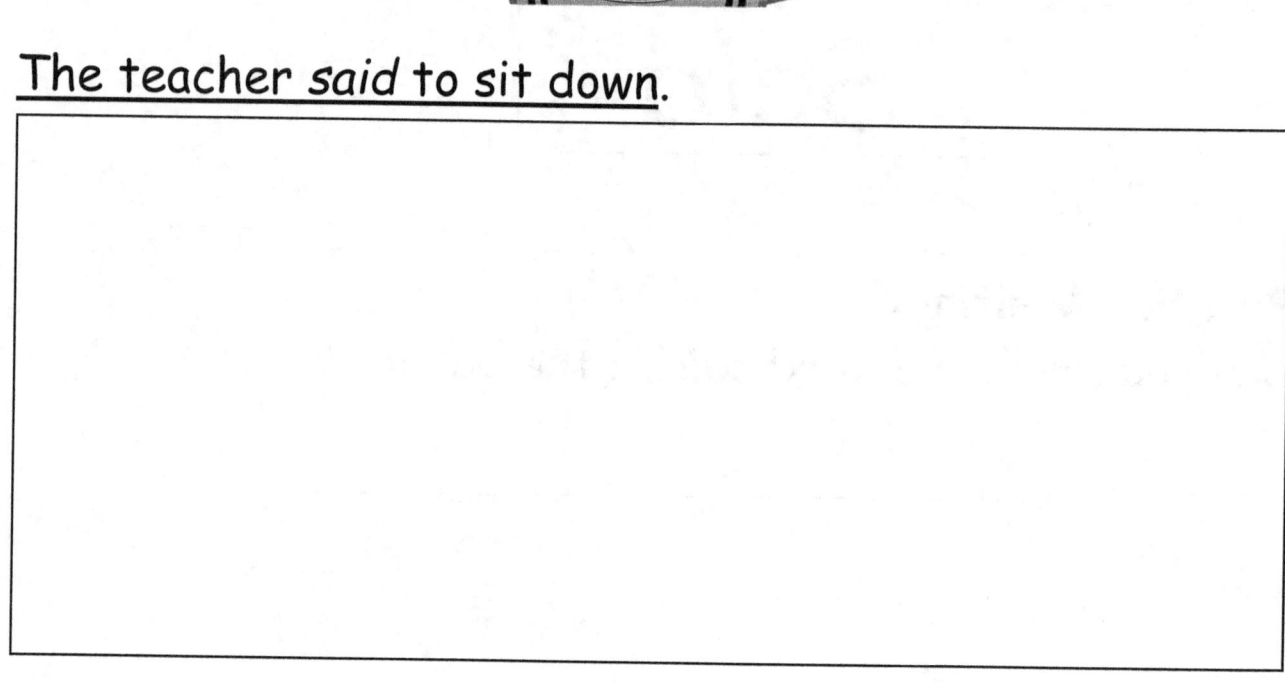

The teacher *said* to sit down.

The little girl *said* to the boy, "Let's play!"

Sight Word:

Here

Practice Writing:

Can you write the word **here** in the box?

Sentence:

We are *here* at the house.

Your turn: Can you write your own sentence using **here**?

Draw It! Read the sentence and draw a picture of it.

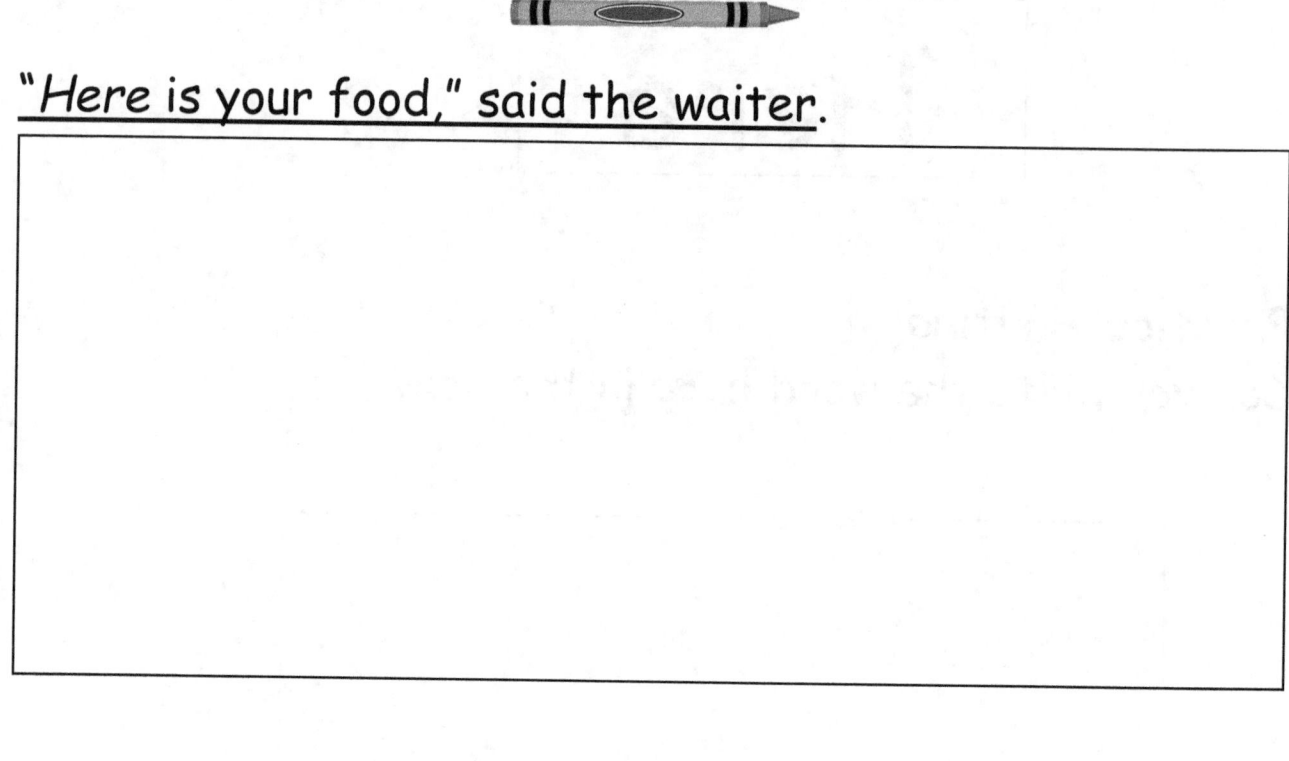

"_Here is your food,_" said the waiter.

"I am _here_ to help you," said the nurse.

Sight Word:

He

Practice Writing:

Can you write the word *he* in the box?

Sentence:

He is my little brother.

Your turn: Can you write your own sentence using *he*?

Draw It! Read the sentence and draw a picture of it.

He likes to jump in the mud.

He plays the drums.

Sight Word:

She

Practice Writing:

Can you write the word **she** in the box?

Sentence:

She is my big sister.

Your turn: Can you write your own sentence using **she**?

Draw It! Read the sentence and draw a picture of it.

She likes to swim in the pool.

She is in the car with her mom.

Sight Word:

Our

Practice Writing:

Can you write the word **our** in the box?

Sentence:

You can come to *our* house.

Your turn: Can you write your own sentence using **our**?

_____

_____

_____

Draw It! Read the sentence and draw a picture of it.

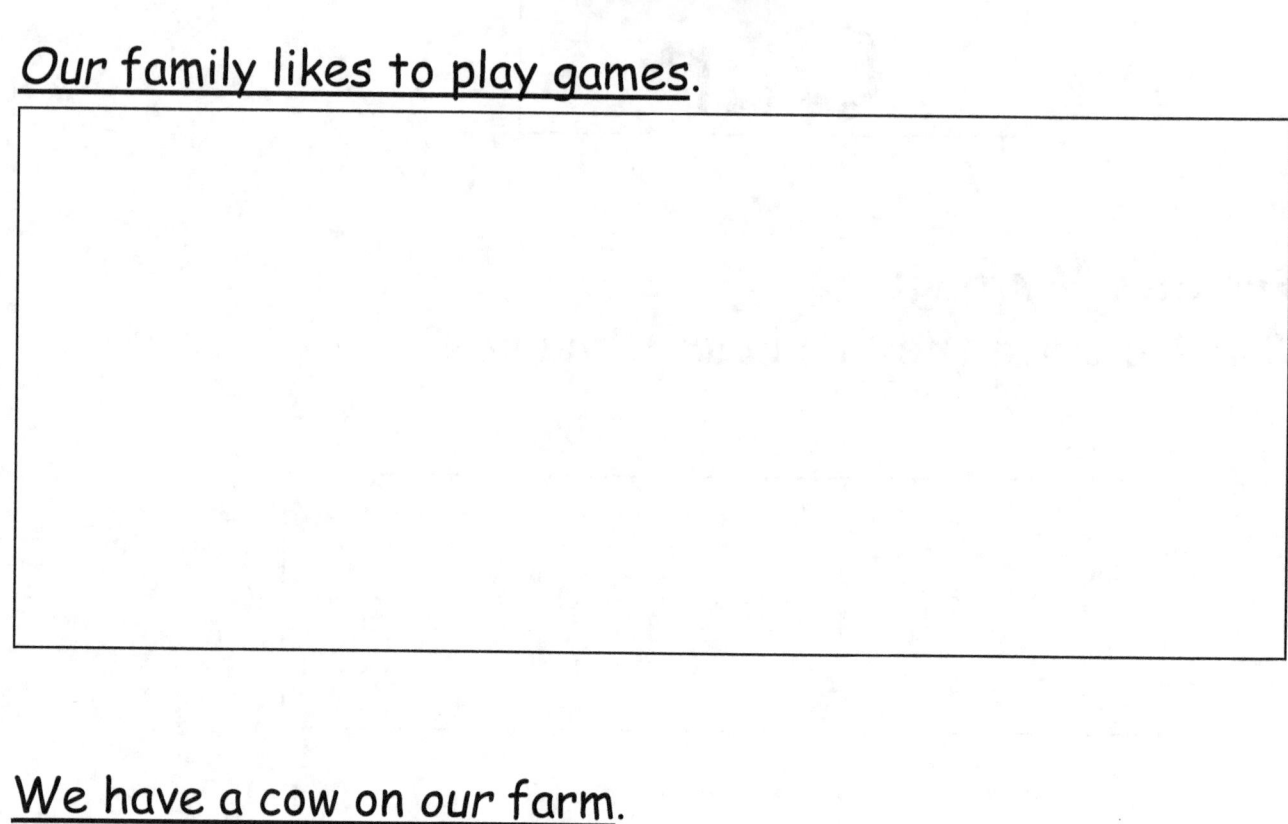

<u>Our family likes to play games</u>.

<u>We have a cow on our farm</u>.

Sight Word:

We

Practice Writing:

Can you write the word **we** in the box?

| |
| |

Sentence:

Will *we* go to the party?

Your turn: Can you write your own sentence using *we*?

Draw It! Read the sentence and draw a picture of it.

<u>We have been friends for a long time</u>.

<u>We take the boat on the lake</u>.

Sight Word:

They

Practice Writing:

Can you write the word **they** in the box?

Sentence:

They went to the car and got inside.

Your turn: Can you write your own sentence using **they**?

Draw It! Read the sentence and draw a picture of it.

<u>They are playing a game of kickball.</u>

<u>They are in a rock and roll band</u>.

Sight Word:

Me

Practice Writing:

Can you write the word **me** in the box?

Sentence:

My friend told *me* to come to her house.

Your turn: Can you write your own sentence using **me**?

Draw It! Read the sentence and draw a picture of it.

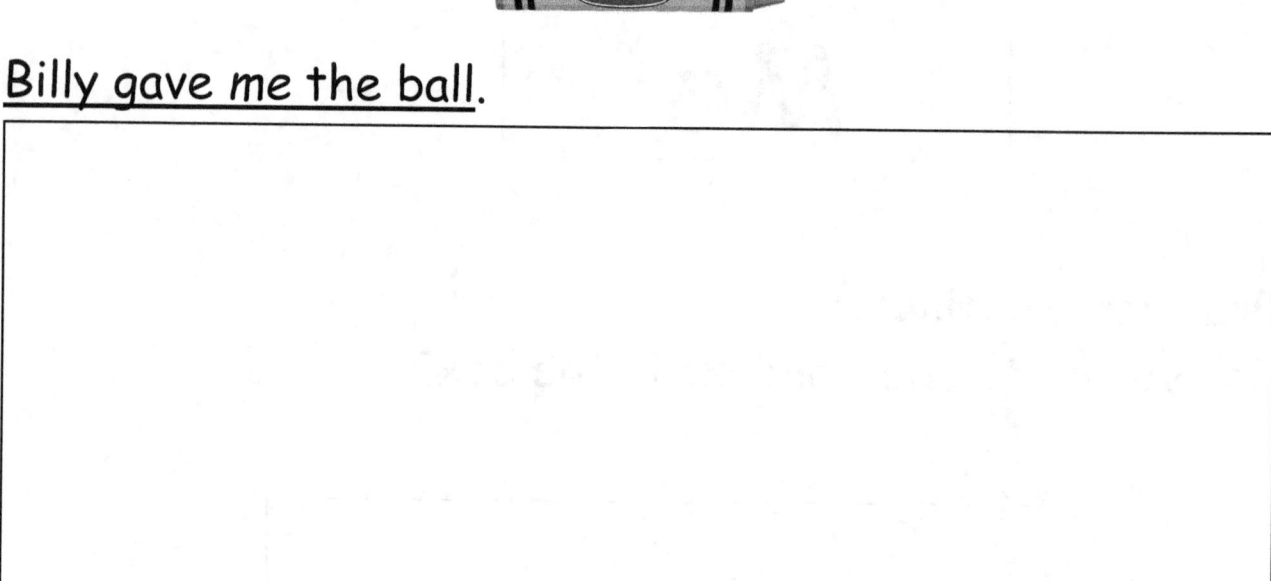

<u>Billy gave *me* the ball</u>.

<u>The stray cat came over to *me*</u>.

Sight Word:

You

Practice Writing:

Can you write the word **you** in the box?

Sentence:

You can have my pen.

Your turn: Can you write your own sentence using **you**?

Draw It! Read the sentence and draw a picture of it.

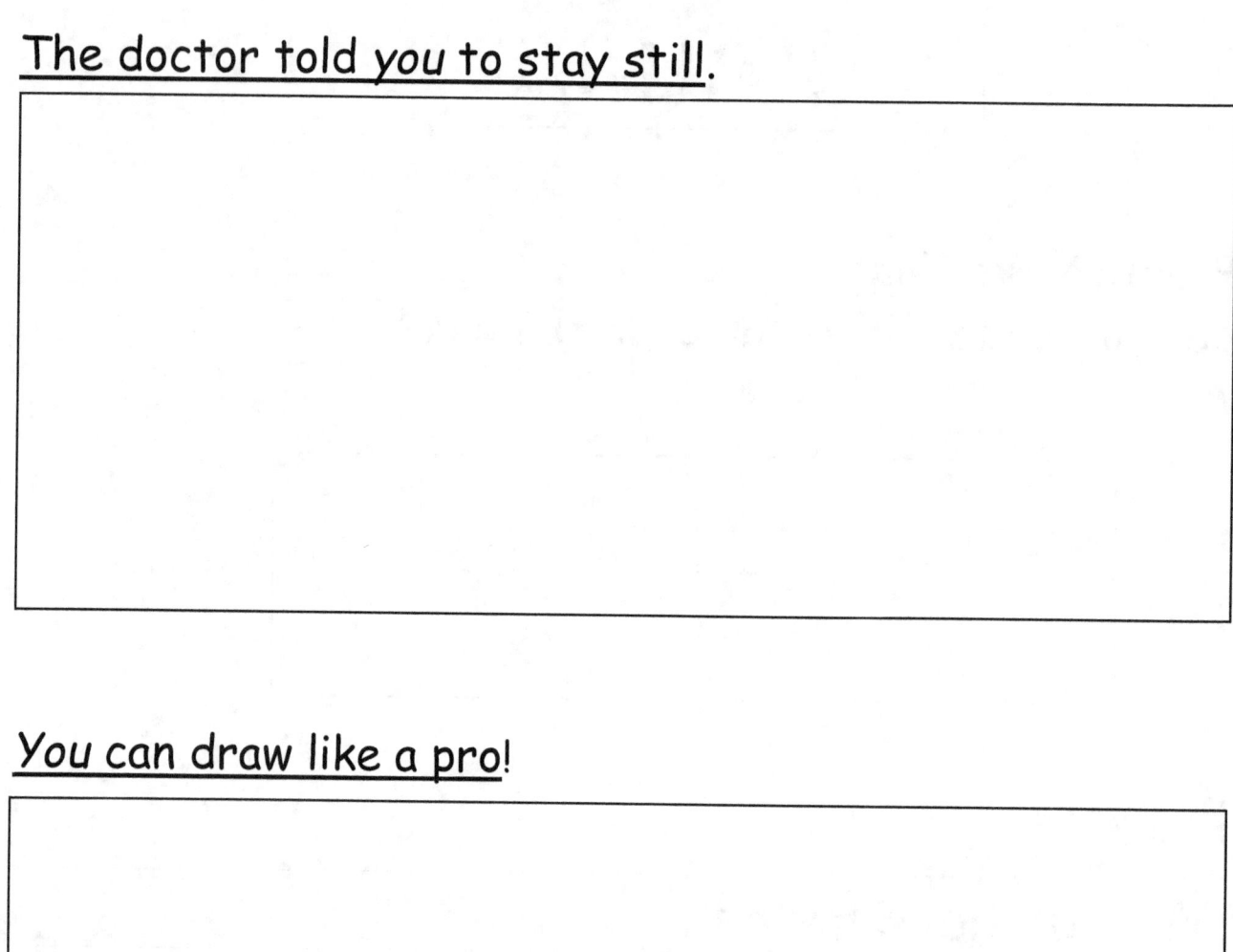

The doctor told <u>you</u> to stay still.

You can draw like a pro!

Sight Word:

This

Practice Writing:

Can you write the word **this** in the box?

Sentence:

This is a picture of my grandpa.

Your turn: Can you write your own sentence using **this**?

Draw It! Read the sentence and draw a picture of it.

This is a picture I drew for you.

I like to wear *this* shirt to school.

Sight Words List 4

Blue
Black
Brown
Red
White
One
Two
Three
Four
To

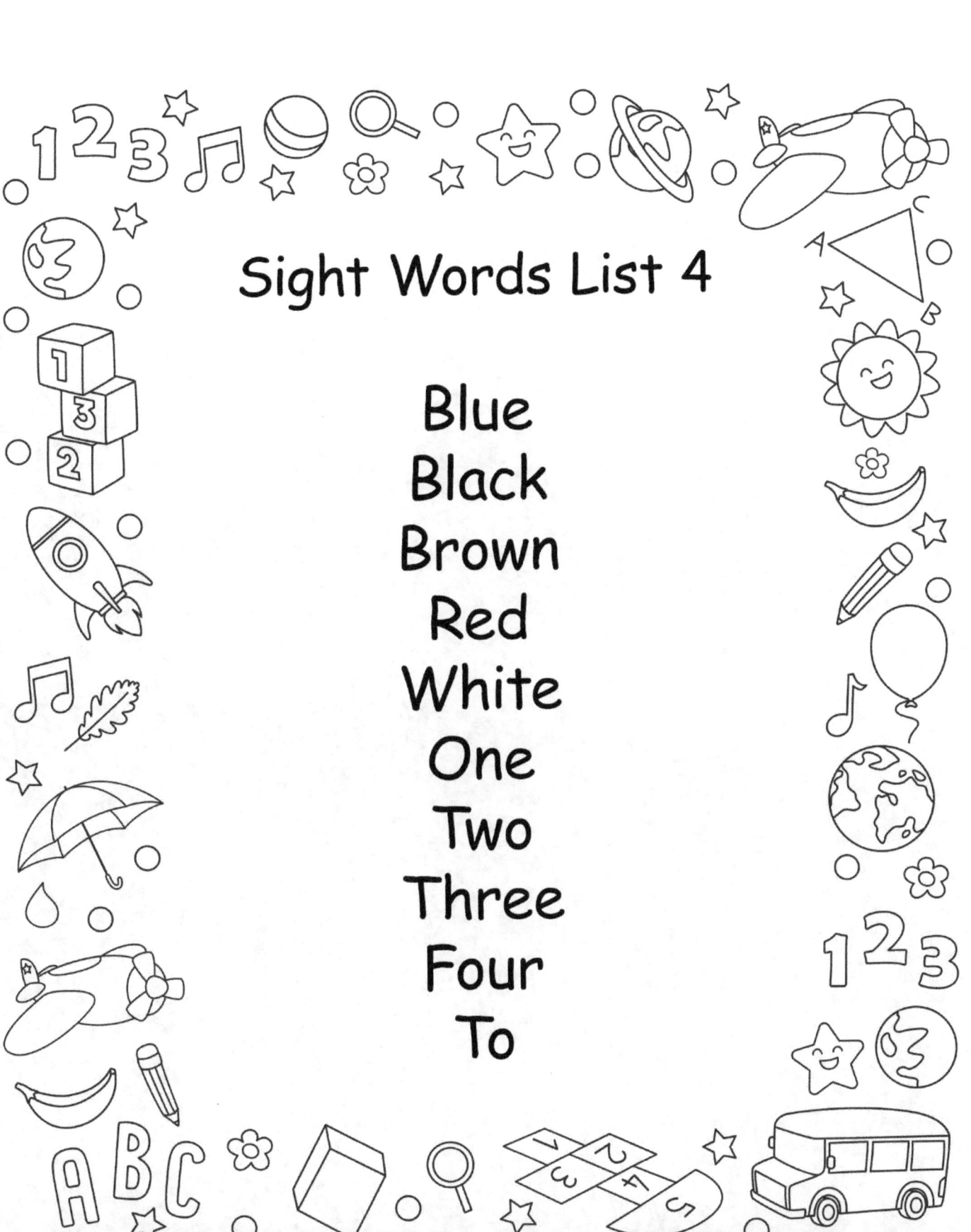

Flashcard Practice:

blue	black
brown	red
white	one

two	three
four	to

Sight Word:

Blue

Practice Writing:

Can you write the word *blue* in the box?

Sentence:

I like to look at the *blue* sky.

Your turn: Can you write your own sentence using *blue*?

Draw It! Read the sentence and draw a picture of it.

<u>My *blue* shirt has dirt on it.</u>

<u>The *blue* car is parked outside.</u>

Sight Word:

Black

Practice Writing:

Can you write the word **black** in the box?

Sentence:

The *black* pen is out of ink.

Your turn: Can you write your own sentence using **black**?

_____

_____

_____

Draw It! Read the sentence and draw a picture of it.

The storm has *black* clouds.

[drawing box]

My teacher has *black* shoes.

[drawing box]

Sight Word:

Brown

Practice Writing:

Can you write the word **brown** in the box?

Sentence:

The *brown* box is on the porch.

Your turn: Can you write a sentence using **brown**?

Draw It! Read the sentence and draw a picture of it.

His _brown_ coat looks warm in the cold.

The _brown_ bug is on my arm.

Sight Word:

Red

Practice Writing:

Can you write the word **red** in the box?

Sentence:

The *red* balloon flew away.

Your turn: Can you write your own sentence using **red**?

Draw It! Read the sentence and draw a picture of it.

We kick the *red* ball in a game of kickball.

My *red* shorts have a rip in them.

Sight Word:

White

Practice Writing:

Can you write the word **white** in the box?

Sentence:

White clouds are my favorite.

Your turn: Can you write a sentence using **white**?

Draw It! Read the sentence and draw a picture of it.

The snow looks like a *white* blanket on the ground.

My *white* socks turned pink in the wash.

Sight Word:

One

Practice Writing:

Can you write the word **one** in the box?

Sentence:

I have *one* brother.

Your turn: Can you write your own sentence using *one*?

Draw It! Read the sentence and draw a picture of it.

There is _one pizza left to eat_.

```
[                                          ]
[                                          ]
[                                          ]
[                                          ]
[                                          ]
[                                          ]
```

I have _one_ dollar in my hand.

```
[                                          ]
[                                          ]
[                                          ]
[                                          ]
[                                          ]
```

Sight Word:

Two

Practice Writing:

Can you write the word **two** in the box?

Sentence:

Two girls sit in the room.

Your turn: Can you write your own sentence using **two**?

Draw It! Read the sentence and draw a picture of it.

I have _two_ flowers to give you.

There are _two_ birds at the window.

Sight Word:

Three

Practice Writing:

Can you write the word *three* in the box?

Sentence:

Can I have *three* dollars for a soda?

Your turn: Can you write a sentence using *three*?

_____

_____

_____

Draw It! Read the sentence and draw a picture of it.

Three boys play a game of soccer.

My sister has *three* dresses.

Sight Word:

Four

Practice Writing:

Can you write the word *four* in the box?

Sentence:

Four of you can play the game.

Your turn: Can you write your own sentence using *four*?

Draw It! Read the sentence and draw a picture of it.

There are *four* gifts under the Christmas tree.

The *four* ants march on the dirt.

Sight Word:

To

Practice Writing:

Can you write the word **to** in the box?

Sentence:

This gift is from me *to* you.

Your turn: Can you write your own sentence using *to*?

_____

_____

_____

Draw It! Read the sentence and draw a picture of it.

<u>I like *to* ride my horse</u>.

<u>We are going *to* my grandma's house</u>.

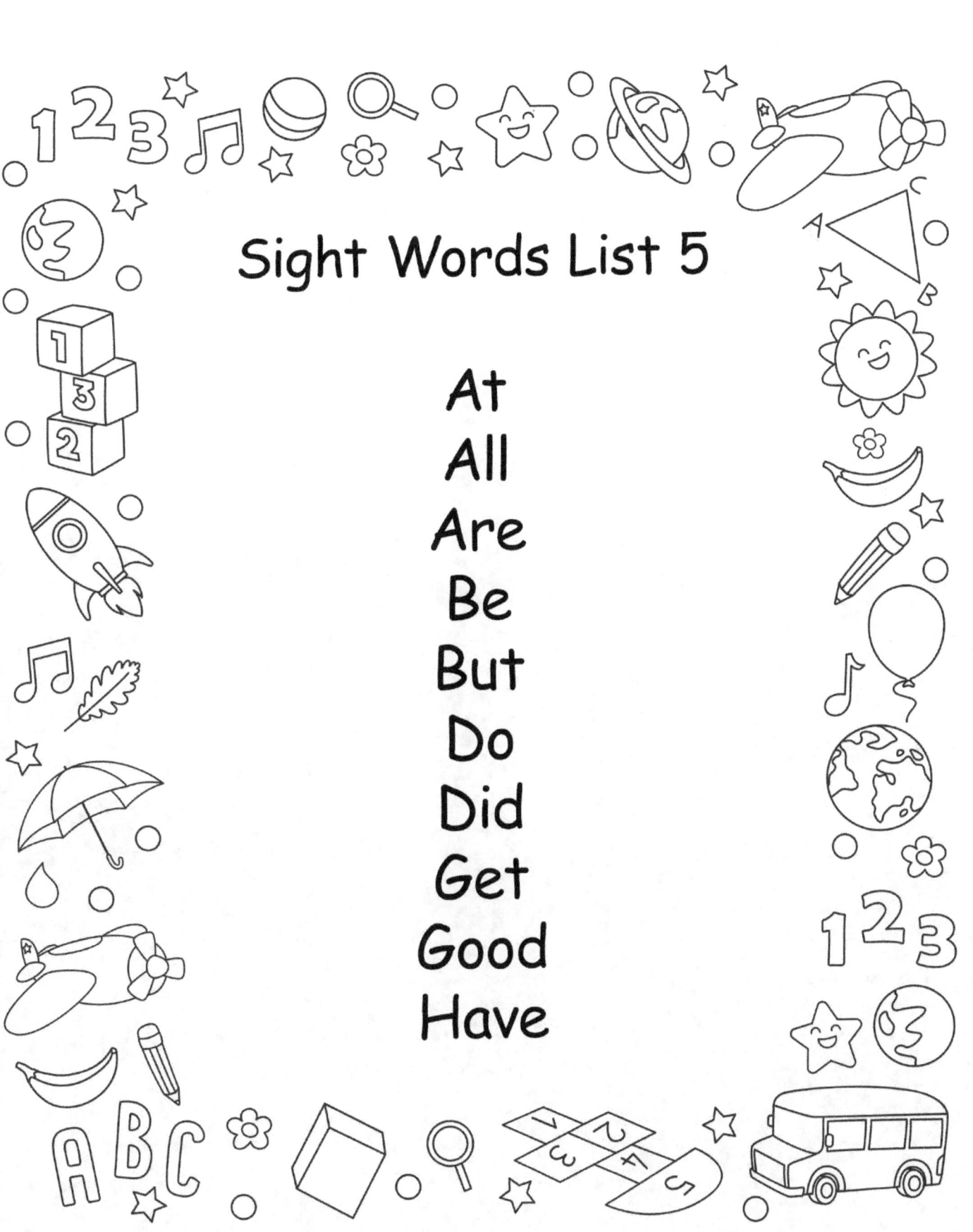

Sight Words List 5

At
All
Are
Be
But
Do
Did
Get
Good
Have

112

Flashcard Practice:

at	all
are	be
but	do

did	get
good	have

Sight Word:

At

Practice Writing:

Can you write the word **at** in the box?

Sentence:

She looks at the picture.

Your turn: Can you write your own sentence using **at**?

Draw It! Read the sentence and draw a picture of it.

We are at the store to buy milk.

I left my shoes at the park.

Sight Word:

All

Practice Writing:

Can you write the word **all** in the box?

Sentence:

All of us want to go with you.

Your turn: Can you write your own sentence using *all?*

Draw It! Read the sentence and draw a picture of it.

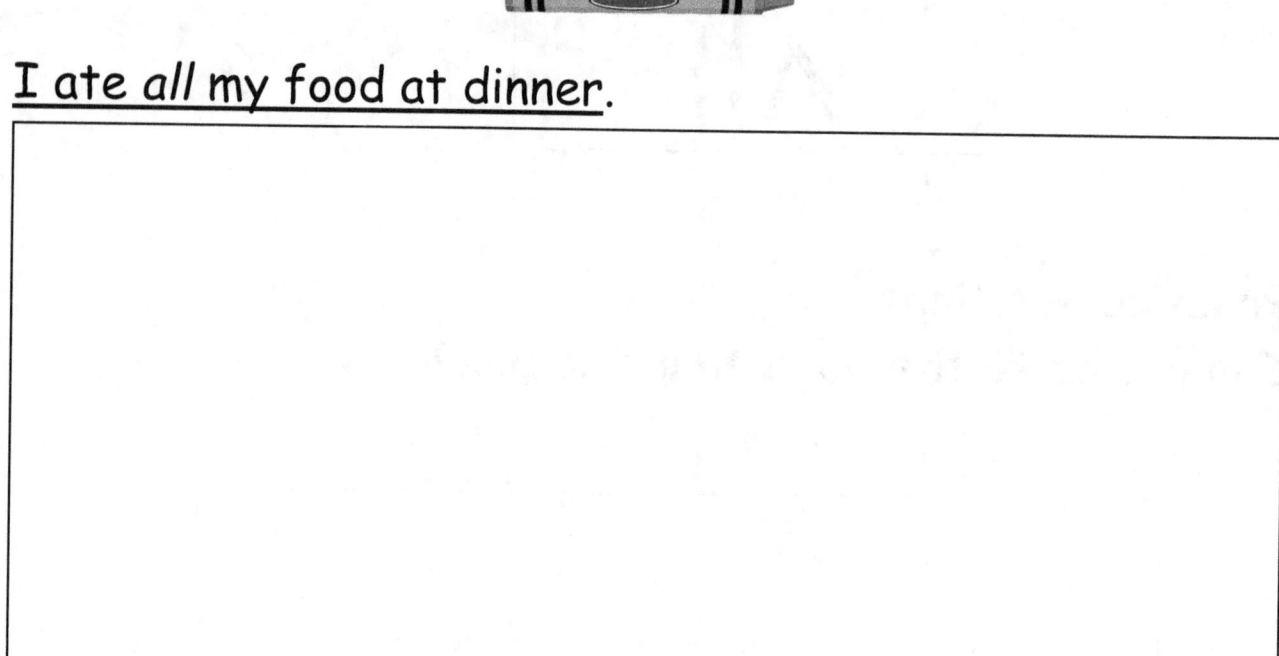

I ate all my food at dinner.

All of the bees are at their hive.

Sight Word:

Are

Practice Writing:

Can you write the word **are** in the box?

Sentence:

Are you going to my house?

Your turn: Can you write your own sentence using **are**?

Draw It! Read the sentence and draw a picture of it.

There are a few cookies left to eat.

We are going to the beach today.

Sight Word:

Be

Practice Writing:

Can you write the word **be** in the box?

Sentence:

There will *be* a game today.

Your turn: Can you write your own sentence using *be*?

Draw It! Read the sentence and draw a picture of it.

The birthday cake will *be* in the shape of a unicorn.

The students are not to *be* outside in the rain.

Sight Word:

But

Practice Writing:

Can you write the word **but** in the box?

Sentence:

She said no, *but* I said yes.

Your turn: Can you write your own sentence using **but**?

_____

_____

_____

Draw It! Read the sentence and draw a picture of it.

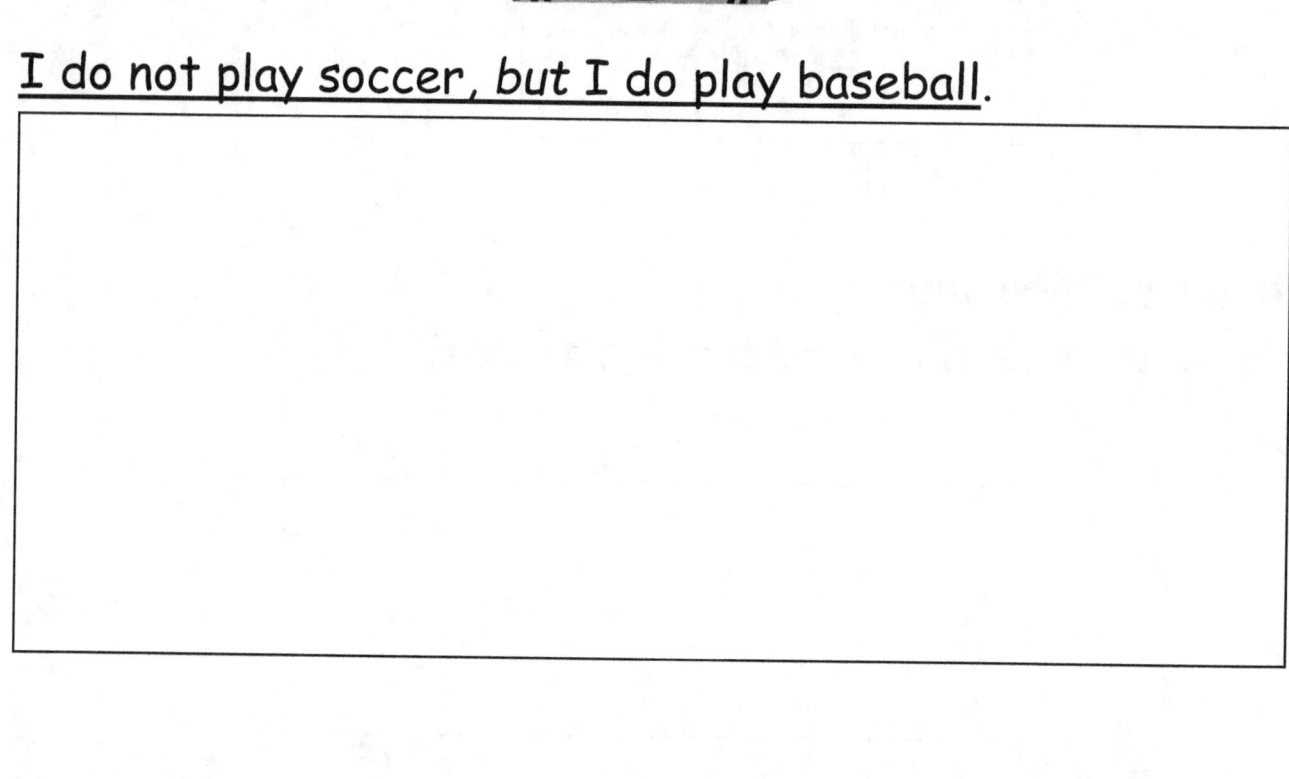

I do not play soccer, *but* I do play baseball.

Her room is messy, *but* she does not like to clean it.

Sight Word:

Do

Practice Writing:

Can you write the word **do** in the box?

Sentence:

I have to *do* my homework.

Your turn: Can you write your own sentence using **do**?

Draw It! Read the sentence and draw a picture of it.

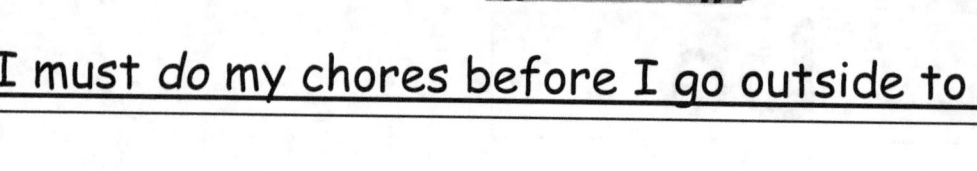

<u>I must *do* my chores before I go outside to play</u>.

```




```

<u>I *do* not like to wake up early</u>.

```




```

Sight Word:

Did

Practice Writing:

Can you write the word *did* in the box?

Sentence:

What *did* you do with my pencil?

Your turn: Can you write your own sentence using *did?*

Draw It! Read the sentence and draw a picture of it.

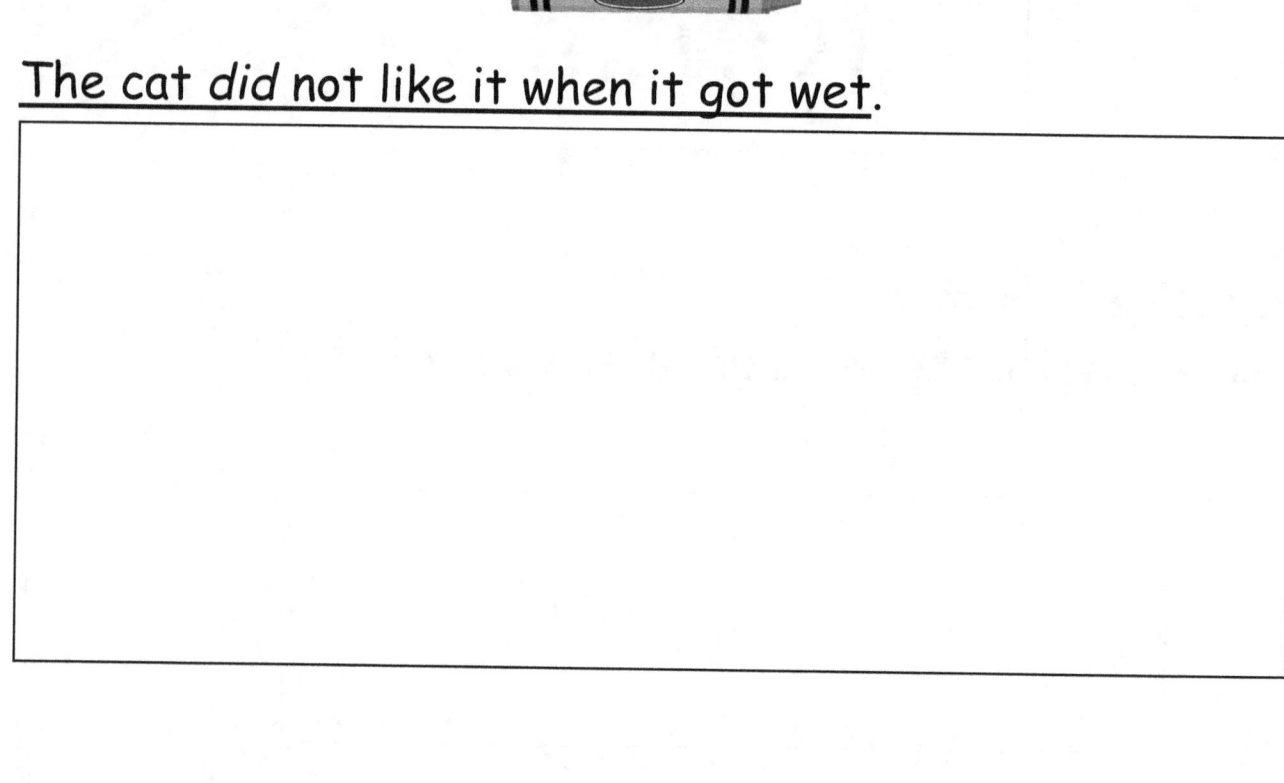

The cat *did* not like it when it got wet.

I *did* not break the vase, but my dog *did*.

Sight Word:

Get

Practice Writing:

Can you write the word *get* in the box?

Sentence:

I *get* to be with my grandpa today.

Your turn: Can you write your own sentence using *get*?

Draw It! Read the sentence and draw a picture of it.

The doctor said I _get_ a sticker for being good.

I _get_ to buy a goldfish today.

Sight Word:

Good

Practice Writing:
Can you write the word *good* in the box?

Sentence:

The team did a *good* job on the field.

Your turn: Can you write your own sentence using *good*?

Draw It! Read the sentence and draw a picture of it.

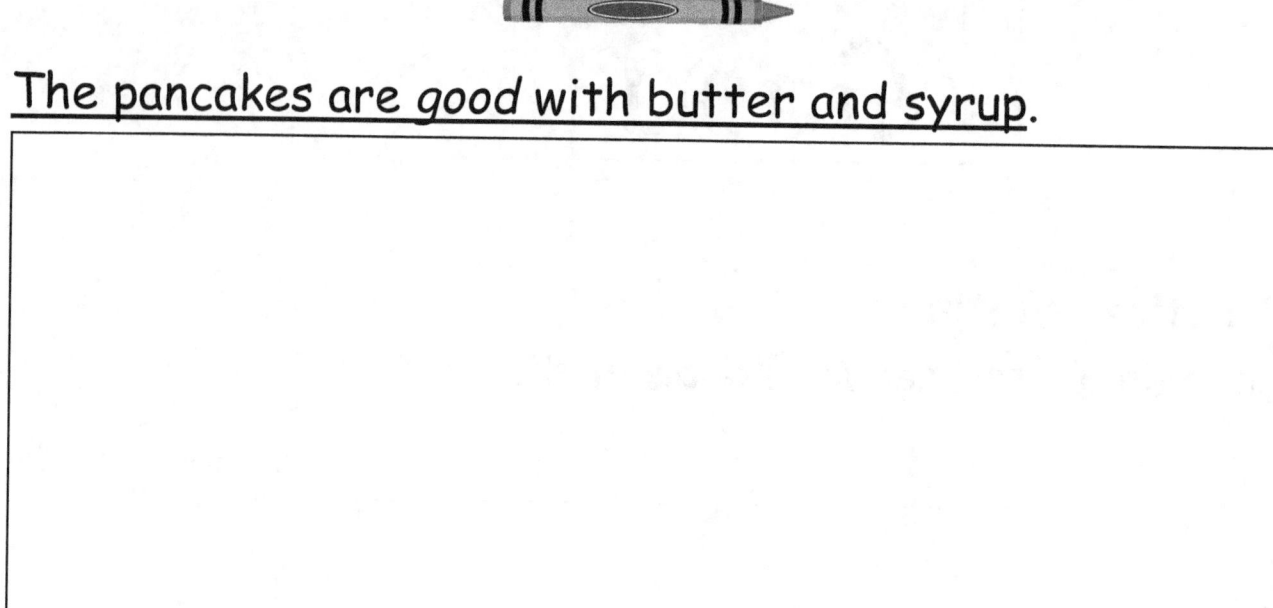

The pancakes are _good_ with butter and syrup.

I feel _good_ and clean after a bath.

Sight Word:

Have

Practice Writing:

Can you write the word **have** in the box?

Sentence:

We have to go home now.

Your turn: Can you write your own sentence using **have**?

Draw It! Read the sentence and draw a picture of it.

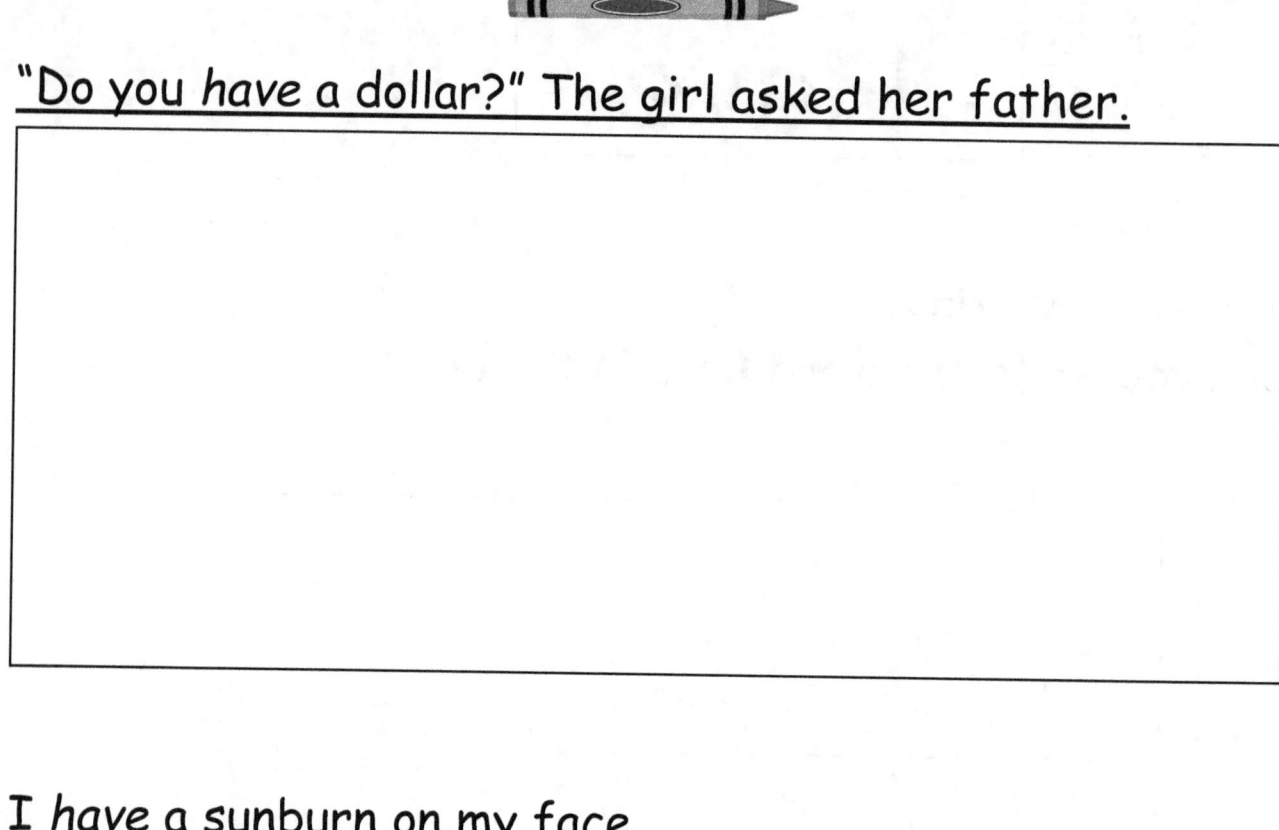

"Do you *have* a dollar?" The girl asked her father.

I *have* a sunburn on my face.

Sight Words List 6

Find
Play
Like
Must
No
Saw
Say
Soon
That
There

Flashcard Practice:

find	play
like	must
no	saw

| say | soon |
| that | there |

Sight Word:

Find

Practice Writing:

Can you write the word *find* in the box?

Sentence:

Can you help me *find* my lost penny?

Your turn: Can you write your own sentence using *find?*

Draw It! Read the sentence and draw a picture of it.

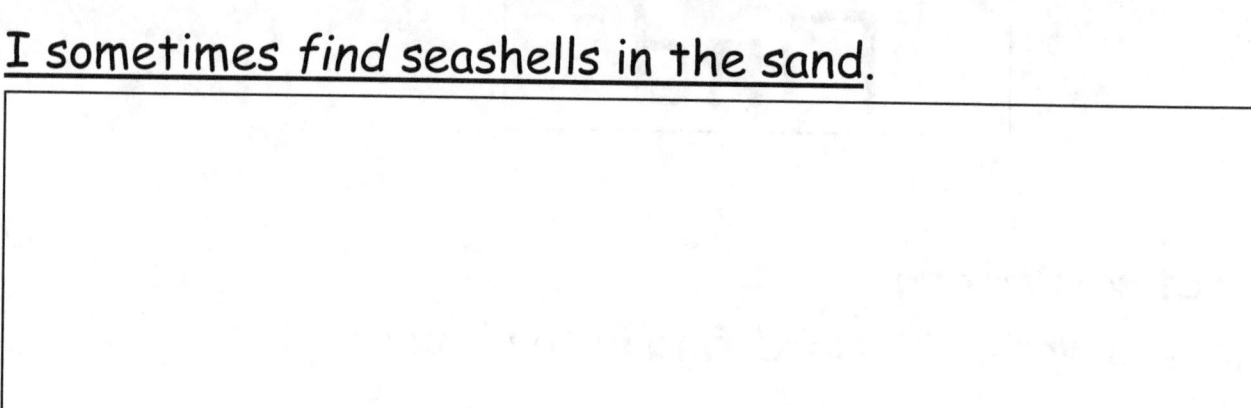

<u>I sometimes *find* seashells in the sand</u>.

<u>We need to *find* a good place to build the fence</u>.

Sight Word:

Play

Practice Writing:

Can you write the word **play** in the box?

Sentence:

I like to *play* with my friends outside.

Your turn: Can you write your own sentence using **play**?

Draw It! Read the sentence and draw a picture of it.

My dog likes to *play* fetch with me.

I *play* dress up with my sister.

Sight Word:

Like

Practice Writing:

Can you write the word *like* in the box?

Sentence:

We *like* to go to the store for ice cream.

Your turn: Can you write your own sentence using *like*?

Draw It! Read the sentence and draw a picture of it.

My father and I like to fix cars.

My mother and I like to sing songs together.

Sight Word:

Must

Practice Writing:

Can you write the word **must** in the box?

Sentence:

We *must* whisper at the movies.

Your turn: Can you write your own sentence using **must**?

Draw It! Read the sentence and draw a picture of it.

Our cat _must_ go to the vet.

I _must_ have ketchup with my French fries.

Sight Word:

No

Practice Writing:

Can you write the word *no* in the box?

Sentence:

There is *no* more milk.

Your turn: Can you write your own sentence using *no*?

Draw It! Read the sentence and draw a picture of it.

There is *no* toothpaste on my toothbrush.

I can have *no* candy until I eat my dinner.

Sight Word:

Saw

Practice Writing:

Can you write the word **saw** in the box?

Sentence:

I *saw* you at the church.

Your turn: Can you write your own sentence using **saw**?

Draw It! Read the sentence and draw a picture of it.

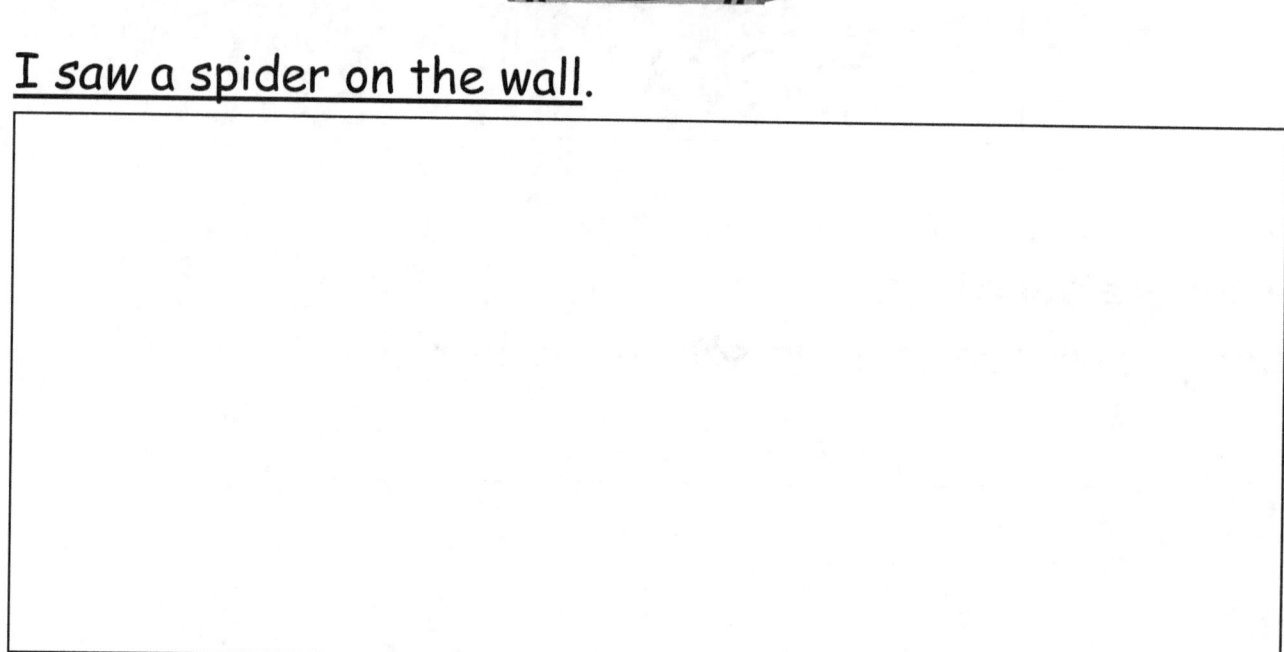

<u>I *saw* a spider on the wall</u>.

<u>My mother saw me hit the ball</u>.

Sight Word:

Say

Practice Writing:

Can you write the word **say** in the box?

Sentence:

What did you *say?*

Your turn: Can you write your own sentence using **say?**

Draw It! Read the sentence and draw a picture of it.

My parents _say_ that I must clean my room to watch T.V.

I _say_ that pizza is the best food ever.

Sight Word:

Soon

Practice Writing:

Can you write the word *soon* in the box?

Sentence:

We need to go home *soon.*

Your turn: Can you write your own sentence using *soon*?

_____

_____

_____

Draw It! Read the sentence and draw a picture of it.

I am happy that the state fair will be here _soon_.

As the days get warmer, we will _soon_ go camping.

Sight Word:

That

Practice Writing:

Can you write the word **that** in the box?

Sentence:

That was nice of you to give your coat.

Your turn: Can you write your own sentence using **that**?

Draw It! Read the sentence and draw a picture of it.

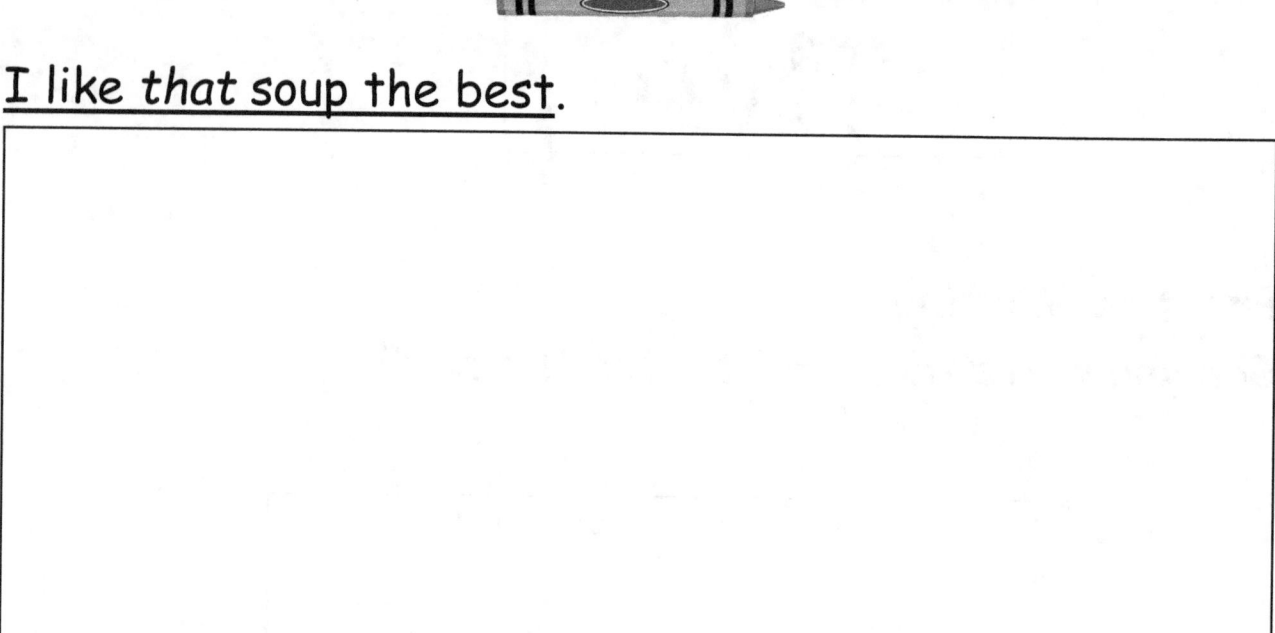

<u>I like *that* soup the best</u>.

┌─────────────────────────────────────┐
│   │
│   │
│   │
│   │
│   │
│   │
└─────────────────────────────────────┘

<u>*That* was a long drive to Florida</u>.

┌─────────────────────────────────────┐
│   │
│   │
│   │
│   │
│   │
│   │
└─────────────────────────────────────┘

Sight Word:

There

Practice Writing:

Can you write the word **there** in the box?

| |
| |

Sentence:

I will go *there* with you.

Your turn: Can you write a sentence using **there**?

Draw It! Read the sentence and draw a picture of it.

<u>There is a fun slide at the park</u>.

<u>When at the zoo, we have fun *there*</u>.

Sight Words List 7

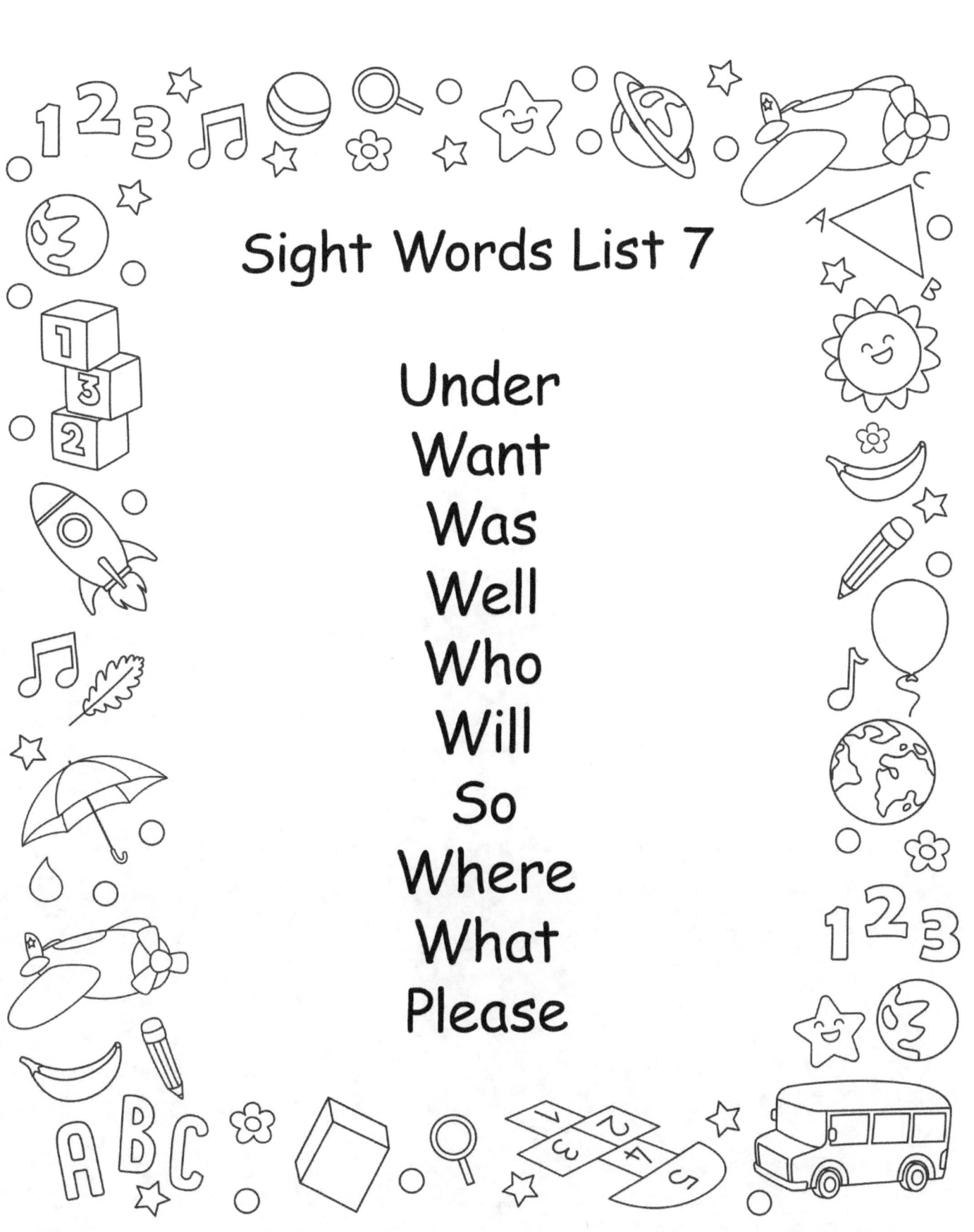

Under
Want
Was
Well
Who
Will
So
Where
What
Please

Flashcard Practice:

under	want
was	well
who	will

so	where
what	please

Sight Word:

Under

Practice Writing:
Can you write the word **under** in the box?

Sentence:

You can find it *under* the desk.

Your turn: Can you write a sentence using **under**?

Draw It! Read the sentence and draw a picture of it.

Our dog hides *under* the bed.

I can swim *under* the water.

Sight Word:

Want

Practice Writing:

Can you write the word **want** in the box?

Sentence:

I want to go with you.

Your turn: Can you write your own sentence using **want**?

Draw It! Read the sentence and draw a picture of it.

The coach said, "Do you *want* to play in the game?"

I *want* yummy cake on my birthday.

Sight Word:

Practice Writing:

Can you write the word **was** in the box?

Sentence:

There *was* an invitation to dinner.

Your turn: Can you write your own sentence using **was**?

Draw It! Read the sentence and draw a picture of it.

The book _was_ on the table where I left it.

The building _was_ on fire.

Sight Word:

Well

Practice Writing:

Can you write the word **well** in the box?

Sentence:

"I am doing *well*," I said to the doctor.

Your turn: Can you write your own sentence using *well?*

Draw It! Read the sentence and draw a picture of it.

My mom was sick, but now she is _well_.

The bucket of water came from the _well_.

Sight Word:

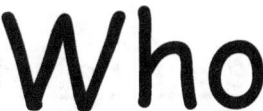

Practice Writing:

Can you write the word **who** in the box?

Sentence:

Who is coming over?

Your turn: Can you write your own sentence using **who**?

Draw It! Read the sentence and draw a picture of it.

The boy *who* is in front of me did not stop talking.

Who made the cookies? They are so good.

Sight Word:

Will

Practice Writing:

Can you write the word **will** in the box?

Sentence:

Will you stop by my house?

Your turn: Can you write your own sentence using _will_?

Draw It! Read the sentence and draw a picture of it.

I _will_ put on my rain boots to play in the puddles.

My mom _will_ pick me up in the van.

Sight Word:

So

Practice Writing:

Can you write the word *so* in the box?

Sentence:

There are *so* many good places to visit.

Your turn: Can you write your own sentence using *so*?

Draw It! Read the sentence and draw a picture of it.

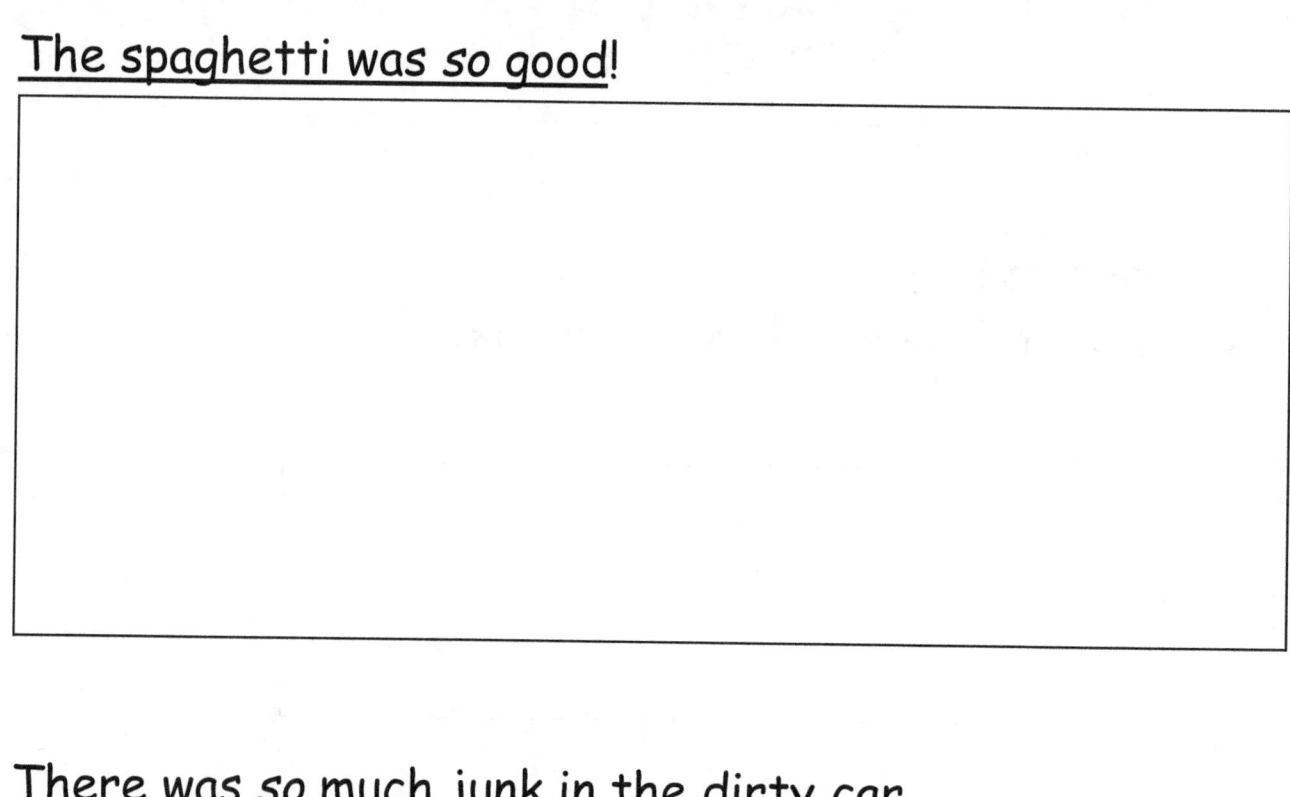

The spaghetti was *so good*!

There was *so* much junk in the dirty car.

Sight Word:

Where

Practice Writing:
Can you write the word **where** in the box?

Sentence:

Where did you go?

Your turn: Can you write a sentence using **where**?

Draw It! Read the sentence and draw a picture of it.

I do not know *where* we are going, but we are on a trip.

My father left the keys *where* he could find them.

Sight Word:

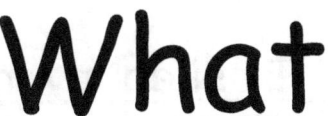

Practice Writing:

Can you write the word **what** in the box?

Sentence:

What is going on here?

Your turn: Can you write your own sentence using **what**?

Draw It! Read the sentence and draw a picture of it.

"_What kind of bug is this?_" I asked my mom.

This is _what_ a pie looks like before it bakes.

Sight Word:

Please

Practice Writing:

Can you write the word **please** in the box?

Sentence:

May I *please* have a turn?

Your turn: Can you write a sentence using **please**?

Draw It! Read the sentence and draw a picture of it.

I say _please_ and thank you when I talk to my parents.

Can there _please_ be a cleanup where the milk spilled?

Sight Words & Sentences is Complete!

Sight Words & Sentences Level 2 is Available Now!

Consider Other Late November Learning Tree Titles:

Journaling for Kids

Journaling is Writing Too!

Journaling through Scripture for Teens

Practicing Poetry

Paragraph Practice

Writing Essays